Empowering You beyond Birthing

Dr Mahima Bakshi is a renowned maternal child wellness consultant, women's rights activist, author of Birthing Naturally and founder-owner of Birthing Naturally Queen. She's a maternity influencer and has been awarded with 'Times Most Influential Personalities 2021' by the Times Group. She has also been felicitated by governors of Maharashtra and Haryana.

She is currently associated as a Maternal Child Consultant with Daffodils by Artemis in Gurugram and Delhi, Sahyadri Hospitals in Pune and Jaslok Hospital in Mumbai. In the past, she has been associated with Fortis Hospitals, Apollo Cradle, Rainbow Children's Hospital and Rosewalk Luxury Hospital for Women.

She is also India's first 'Dancing for Birth' certified instructor. She has completed certification courses in International Women's Health and Human Rights from Stanford University; Global Adolescent Health from University of Melbourne; Everyday Parenting as well as Global Quality Maternal and Newborn Care from Yale University; Perinatal Mental Health from Postpartum Support International, USA. She has also completed advanced certified Lactation Professional India programme and has received certification in 'Breastfeeding and Breast Diseases' from Federation of Obstetric and Gynaecological Societies of India. She has also been certified as a birth doula and water birth coach by Waterbirth International.

She completed her master's in Reproductive Child Health Management from United Nations International Children's Emergency Fund and Maternal Infant Young Child Adolescent Nutrition Course from Public Health Foundation of India.

Empowering You beyond Birthing

A GUIDE FOR NEW PARENTS ON POSTNATAL
WELL-BEING AND EQUAL PARENTING

Mahima Bakshi

Published by
Rupa Publications India Pvt. Ltd 2022
7/16, Ansari Road, Daryaganj
New Delhi 110002

Sales centres:
Allahabad Bengaluru Chennai
Hyderabad Jaipur Kathmandu
Kolkata Mumbai

Copyright © Mahima Bakshi 2022

The views and opinions expressed in this book are the
author's own and the facts are as reported by her which
have been verified to the extent possible, and the publishers
are not in any way liable for the same.

All rights reserved.
No part of this publication may be reproduced, transmitted,
or stored in a retrieval system, in any form or by any means,
electronic, mechanical, photocopying, recording or otherwise,
without the prior permission of the publisher.

ISBN: 978-93-5520-446-2

First impression 2022

10 9 8 7 6 5 4 3 2 1

The moral right of the author has been asserted.

Printed in India

This book is sold subject to the condition that it shall not,
by way of trade or otherwise, be lent, resold, hired out, or otherwise
circulated, without the publisher's prior consent, in any form of
binding or cover other than that in which it is published.

Contents

Preface — vii

Introduction — xi

1. During the Hospital Stay after Delivery — 1
2. Breastfeed: Your Child's First Feed after Birth — 6
3. The Art of Breastfeeding — 11
4. Modern-Day Parenting the Traditional Way — 19
5. Preventing Post-Partum Depression — 31
6. Me Time — 37
7. Making Your Child Independent without Getting Detached — 43
8. Playtime with Your Baby — 52
9. Getting Back in Shape — 60

10. Complementary Feed	69
11. Impact of Couple's Relationship on the Baby	76
12. Working Parents	83
13. Be the Baby	92
14. From First to Second Year	97
15. Mindful Parenting	102
16. Avoiding Another Pregnancy Too Soon	110
17. Skin and Hair Care	117
18. Rediscovering Your Inner Goddess	122
Afterword	126
Acknowledgements	129

Preface

To cope better with the birthing process, it is important that you and your partner begin preparing right from the pregnancy phase. This will help you bond with the baby as well as with each other. It also makes you ready for taking up shared responsibilities, improving your lifestyle, learning the basics of parenting and rearranging the priorities in your life as you head towards parenthood.

Equal partnership from both is essential in letting the baby know that both the parents are equally excited for their arrival and are doing their best to welcome them into this world in the most natural way. Preparing yourself for a natural childbirth is helpful. *Birthing Naturally,* my first book, is a pregnancy wellness guide to help expecting couples prepare themselves mentally and physically for natural birthing by helping them improve their lifestyle and more.

Let your pregnancy be the healthiest phase of your life—make lifestyle changes together, enjoy the pregnancy together, make memories and prepare for childbirth together.

As we live in this new era of gender equality, you also need to head towards equal parenting for better growth and development of your baby through the early years. You need to help prepare yourself for the journey after your baby's birth.

Many women end up with post-partum depression and suffer a feeling of loss of identity while taking care of their baby. This book will assist women in understanding how they can take care of their health and as well as of their baby. However, partner support is equally important in making this happen. Hence, this book emphasizes on equal parenting to help the partner get more involved in taking care of the baby and sharing responsibilities. Parenting begins right from the pregnancy by being equally involved in taking care of the baby. A husband must accompany his wife for her scans and check-up, attend prenatal sessions with her and prepare for childbirth together. Dads can bond with the unborn by talking to the belly, cuddling the mother, practising prenatal exercises together, giving her massages when she is tired and be her labour support partner. The change should begin right during pregnancy.

When both partners are equally involved in taking care of the baby and each other, the entire journey from pregnancy to parenthood becomes smoother. It is not just the preparation up to the birth of your baby that holds significance but also how you look after them once they are born. This book will help couples get ready for their journey towards parenthood, which starts beyond birthing.

Introduction

Being a new parent comes with a lot of challenges, especially when it is your first time. These involve adapting to a new life while taking care of a new life—your little one. You might experience a rollercoaster ride with your newborn—with the constant crying, the frequent demands for feed, doctor's visits, vaccinations and lots more.

This book will help couples understand how they can together give the best to their little one, right from the very beginning. Parenthood is not easy, but when done right, it can positively impact your child's future.

The initial period of your newborn's life is a very important stage for building their immunity. Natural childbirth exposes the baby to the microbiomes present in the birth canal. A baby picks up their immunity from there too. Post birth, a baby gets immunity boost from the mother's milk—the initial milk, colostrum—and even from her skin, both being rich in antibodies.

Read this book to understand how you can provide the best for your baby, be it in terms of their well-being or their growth and development in the face of the existing challenges that the modern society can put you through. You will understand how to handle your baby, how to make them emotionally independent and how to put quality efforts in shaping their personality and health, both physical and mental.

Equal attention needs to be given to maternal well-being too. This book will aid new mothers in taking care of their postnatal health and gradually rediscover themselves.

This book will be of assistance when it comes to taking care of your post-partum health. It will also broaden your understanding of equal parenting. It will help men realize the importance of their support that is needed to improve the maternal child health status around us.

1

During the Hospital Stay after Delivery

It is a very magical moment—the first sight of your baby, the first time you smell the little munchkin, the first time you feel their skin against your hands, the first time they look at you—when your little bundle of joy in front of you. It is a moment mixed with emotions, tough to be explained in words. You are tired after giving birth, but excited and nervous to see and hold them. You feel emotional thinking that you indeed made them.

Right when you hold your little one in your arms, make a promise to yourself as a new parent. This is for the mother as well as the father. Tell yourself that you would do everything to not just give the best of the materialistic world to your baby, but also the best of health, the best of care, the best of your quality time, the best support and the best of your attention as they grow, starting right from their schooldays to beyond. As you hold them for the first time, whisper into their ears that they are in the safest hands. Let them know that you would do everything to take care of them physically, mentally, emotionally or spiritually.

Let the newborn be placed on your chest with their skin touching yours. Let them feel the smell and the warmth of your body. This skin-to-skin contact is important. While it does help in better breastfeeding, it also makes your baby feel emotionally secure. That's your bonding time with your little one.

Not just the mother, the father too should do it. Hold them close to your body. They're going to love it. Your body warmth will also help in maintaining their body temperature. Mothers have already bonded with their babies while carrying them in their wombs. Fathers, too, need to bond—so try the magic of skin-to-skin. You should also learn how to change diapers and help the baby burp. You can sing some lullabies to your newborn and learn how to calm them down when they turn cranky.

The newborn should sleep next to the mother. I refer to it as co-sleeping, where the mother and the baby sleep together. Let the baby take in your smell and let your body feel the baby next to you. It helps in stimulating hormones for lactation too. Knowing that you are right next to them also provides an emotional security to the baby. Avoid sending them to the nursery the very first night even if you are exhausted due to the labour or caesarean (C-section) birth. With the baby sleeping next to you, you will be able to tend to their needs on time.

First night could be easy or rough, but you need to be mentally prepared for both. Don't forget that it is their first night too, outside your womb. You would still be learning from the hospital staff and family about how to look after the little one. You would basically be changing their diaper or feeding them when they are hungry. Rest of the time, they would be mostly sleeping. Avoid meeting too many relatives in the first two days at the hospital as you need to catch up on rest whenever your little one dozes off. Since it is going to be tiring, you both would need rest. I always suggest my patients to only allow the closest of family members to visit them at the hospital and meet everyone else once they go back home. That way, they would be able to get more rest and sleep at the hospital, and, hence, recover faster and feel fresher.

Many people nowadays opt for birth photography or photoshoots for their newborn. You can capture the memories and preserve those forever—your child will cherish those once they grow up. Those pictures can always go into that baby booklet that you have been preparing since your pregnancy.

When it comes to lactating at the hospital in the initial days, it can be challenging, but is a great time to learn and practise with the help of the lactation team around. Start preparing yourself for it right from your pregnancy—read about it and attend workshops. It is not going to be easy, but lactation has many benefits. I will talk about the same in the next chapter.

Many families, especially in India, follow some cultural beliefs that do not carry any scientifically proven benefits—giving honey to the newborn being one such example. Try to make a list of all the cultural traditions that your family might be interested in following once your baby arrives and raise those with your doctor to identify which ones are actually beneficial for your baby and which ones are plain myths.

Don't forget that your baby is dependent on you and would need you to do the best for them. They expect you to ensure that you would not allow traditions, based on no scientific backing, to negatively impact their health. If needed, you may ask your doctor to counsel your family against following the traditions that you do not deem healthy for the baby.

To ensure that you get good facilities and services during your hospital stay, you can check with the hospital concerned before making your bookings. It is, in fact, better to choose your hospital keeping the services in mind as it will help in making your stay smoother post delivery.

During the Hospital Stay after Delivery

There are many hospitals that provide additional services after delivery helps in easier recovery. Check with a few hospitals around you before selecting one.

Dear Mom,

Giving birth to your little one is God's way of empowering you. Once you transition into this new phase motherhood, you will feel stronger from within. It's just like a rebirth—with the birth of your baby, you too are being born again, as a mother. Your life would change but everything will be worthwhile. Just believe in yourself, follow your instincts and do what is being advised for the benefit of your body and your baby. Gradually, you will be able to take up the new role in a beautiful way just like you took up the role of being a partner earlier.

Love,

Dr Mahima Bakshi

2

Breastfeed: Your Child's First Feed after Birth

When it comes to feeding your little one, there are many options you can choose from. While some might suggest opting for formula feed, some might give preference to expressed feed. Remember, World Health Organization (WHO) recommends exclusive breastfeeding for the first six months.[1] The important question here is how to decide. Speak to your doctor about it and stay in touch with a lactation expert.

Breastfeeding needs to be initiated as soon as possible

---

[1] 'Exclusive breastfeeding for six months best for babies everywhere', World Health Organization, 15 January 2011, https://bit.ly/3MGc8SS. Accessed on 23 May 2022.

after the delivery. The golden period is within one to two hours of natural delivery and four to six hours of a C-section. Breastfeeding can prove to be very challenging for some mothers, especially those who have undergone a C-section, as the stitches restrict movement. You will have to be extremely patient. Also, don't forget that your baby can take time to learn. So, it is absolutely okay if a few feeds don't go well in the initial days. Just keep practising and let your baby try.

Breastfeed whenever your baby needs it. Watch for the hunger cues—when your baby is hungry, they would try to make lip smacking sounds, put their hand into their mouth or try to open their mouth and move their neck towards left or right trying to search for your breast. These signs mean that your baby is ready for their next feed. In case you don't pay attention to these on time, they might get cranky and start crying—their way of telling you that they are hungry.

First, calm down your baby and then help them latch on to your breast. Try to pay attention to the early hunger signs and feed them on time to ensure they do not turn excessively cranky. It can take you some time to understand the different tones of your baby's cry. Check the diaper. They might be feeling too hot or too cold, might be gassy or just in need of some attention. If the baby does not feed for as long as two to three hours during the initial days, it is best to wake them up and try to feed them. Long gaps between two feeds need to be avoided. Frequent feeding also helps in enhancing the milk supply and in preventing engorgement by emptying the breast on time.

You would be getting loads of different suggestions from different people. Remember, just because something worked for someone's baby, doesn't mean it is advisable to be followed for your baby too. Listen to what your doctors tell you rather than getting carried away by too many suggestions. Not doing so will lead to confusion and you will lose the confidence to bring up your own baby, especially if you are a first-time parent. Following what your lactation expert teaches you would be the best. Practise breastfeeding your baby in their presence before you get discharged from the hospital and stay in touch with them even after you get back home. Your baby would show growth spurts around two weeks, two to three months and six months. Your baby would keep demanding feed all the time during the growth spurt. It can be very tiring and stressful, so meet your lactation expert at these stages. They will guide you on how to manage the feeds as well as your baby.

While breastfeeding, it is important for new mothers to know that they are doing it right, so that the confusion as a result of too many suggestions can be avoided. During the early days, only allow your lactation expert to be around you while you breastfeed. Tell your husband that you expect some privacy at home while breastfeeding during the early days as you want to practise and gain the confidence. Lesser the number of people who watch you breastfeed, lesser the number of suggestions. And once you have mastered the art of breastfeeding through practice and with the help of your lactation expert, you will feel more confident about doing it the right way. Thereafter, the uncalled-for suggestions wouldn't affect you much.

You also need to ensure that your baby gains proper weight for which they must get foremilk and hindmilk, as both are important. Foremilk is richer in water and is released in about the first 10 minutes of the feed. It helps the baby in maintaining hydration. Hindmilk starts getting released 10 minutes after the foremilk and is richer in fat, protein, carbs and vitamins. Hence, to ensure that your baby gets both, you must breastfeed for at least 15–20 minutes on one side, and shift to the other breast only when the baby does not seem to be full. It also helps in preventing breast engorgement.

In the early days, you might face issues with producing milk, especially if you are a first-time mother. Remember that frequent breastfeeding is what will help in initiating the milk release. So whether there is milk or not, put the baby to your breast when they are hungry and try feeding.

Dear Mom,

Everyone is going to tell you that 'breast milk is the best feed for your baby.' There could be initial challenges wherein your body might struggle in adapting into the post-partum phase. You might experience breast changes and have sore nipples, but remember every drop of your milk is elixir for your baby. So don't give up, no matter how hard it seems initially. Remember, it only gets easier and simpler with time.

Keep trying and keep believing in yourself, you can do it!

Love,

Dr Mahima Bakshi

3

The Art of Breastfeeding

Breastfeeding in the beginning can be very challenging. Preparing yourself for the same by attending workshops in your third trimester will help you understand and learn the basics. You will be able to mentally prepare yourself for the challenges that you might face in the initial days post delivery.

Remember, it's not just new for you but also for your little one. Hence, 'patience' is the keyword to master the art of breastfeeding. You need your me time with your baby in which you can practise and bond with them. You will gain the confidence to hold and position them right, to help them latch on and unlatch the correct way and to burp them properly. It's okay if you take time to learn. Follow up with your lactation expert to understand how to do it right, if you fear you aren't.

Try to avoid too many suggestions from family or friends on how to feed. Let this be between you, your baby and your doctors. It can take about three to five days initially for you to establish breastfeed properly. This is the time where you need to stay focused. Don't give up and stay patient. Your little one can throw tantrums and have mood swings in the beginning, but that is okay. You will gradually understand how to look after them.

There might be times when you'd want to rest for a while. However, stay put from giving formula feed to the baby on your own. It is the exclusive breastfeeding in the early days that plays the most significant role in maintaining the health of your baby. You can manually express milk or pump it out when you feel exhausted or unwell. The expressed feed can be given to the baby using a feeding cup by the father. This way your baby will still get your breast milk.

Frequent Breastfeeding Is the Key to Establishing a Good Breastfeed

Many moms stress out a lot if they are not able to establish breastfeed right on the first day or if there is any medical condition due to which the baby has to be kept in the nursery for a longer time. Stress further affects the milk production and thus the breastfeeding. So, stay calm and relaxed. Seek help from your lactation expert if need be. Proper rest, soft music, lots of water to drink and affection from partner can help in preventing post-delivery distress.

Some women go through post-traumatic stress disorder or birth trauma where due to a difficult or prolonged labour, they get flashbacks of the hardships faced even after delivery. This kind of stress can also delay lactation.

Family members must ensure that they give proper attention, affection, physical support to a new mother. Allow her to have proper rest. It will help in stimulating the happy hormones in her body and hence reduce the stress levels.

Talk to your baby's paediatrician to understand whether your little one weighs alright. Let the doctor decide whether any additional or reduced feeding is needed. Please don't start formula feed on your own just because your baby cries a lot or your family members tell you that your feed is not sufficient. If such a situation arises, meet your lactation expert as well as your baby's paediatrician, who can together help you ensure that you carry on with breastfeeding in an effective manner. Most babies lose some weight in the beginning. Also, the baby must urinate at least four to six times a day. Keeping these two factors in mind, one can gauge whether the baby is being breastfed well or not.

WHO says if an additional feed must be given to your little one, and if you are not able to breastfeed, then preference must given to a donor's milk.[2] There are many human milk banks that provide donor's milk. It is a better option than the formula feeds available in markets. Speak with your doctor about it.

Don't hesitate in asking for help from the hospital staff or your family members. Ensure you sit in the right posture to prevent backaches as a result of breastfeeding. I strongly recommend all new mothers to use a feeding pillow. Keep an additional pillow behind your back for extra support. Remember to bring the baby up to your breasts instead of bending forward. Instead of feeding on the bed, I always recommend my patients to sit upright on a comfortable chair to feed, using the armrest and the footrest.

Position the baby in the right way—it could be football hold, cross cradle or cradle in the sitting position. Learn about holding your baby in all positions from the hospital staff before getting discharged. The same position need not be used for both sides while breastfeeding the baby. See which position your little one prefers on each side.

Ensure the baby has properly latched on to your breast. Not just the nipple, but some part of the areola too must go inside the baby's mouth. The nipple should be deeply seated above the baby's tongue. Their lips should be curled outwards, with the chin touching the breast.

A nursing bra helps prevent sagging of the breasts as

---

[2]https://bit.ly/3ai5Evi. Accessed on 23 May 2022.

well as backache. Your breast size can change. Hence, you must ensure that you change the bra size accordingly—it should not be too tight.

I strongly advise my patients to massage their breasts before bath with olive oil—in a clockwise and anticlockwise motion, 10 times each, applying pressure from the palm. It also helps in self-examination and maintaining blood circulation. If you feel there are lumps or hardness with excessive pain in the breasts, please go meet your lactation expert. Nipple soreness develops when the baby has been latching on to your breasts in an incorrect way. Best way to prevent this is to ensure that the baby latches on correctly. Also, your own expressed milk can be very beneficial in healing your nipples, as it carries antibacterial properties. Ensure you don't apply any soap on your nipples while taking a bath. Just clean them with warm water. You may just stand under the shower for a while. It helps in hot fomentation. Icepacks can also be applied on the nipples after feeding.

After some time you might experience milk ejection reflex—your nipples might start leaking on the sight or sound of your baby. It's a good sign for it means that the milk is flowing well. You can use breast pads to prevent staining of clothes. It must be changed every four to five hours. Allow some air circulation around the nipples and don't keep them padded all the time. Pure lanolin creams are good for treating sore nipples.

Burp them up: Don't forget every feed must be followed by burping. It helps in releasing the excess air that your little one might have taken in while being fed. It also helps in preventing colicky pain. Even if the baby doesn't burp immediately, hold the baby in a burping position for at least the next 15 minutes before putting them down. While putting down your baby, ensure their head is slightly elevated, as it helps in releasing any trapped air.

Pump it out: If the baby is unable to feed through your breast or if you are unable to breastfeed, then you may express the milk using a breast pump or manual expression. Manual expression can be very tiring and lengthy and, thus, electric pumps could be a better option. There are pumps with stimulation techniques that help in maintaining milk supply. Don't forget that direct breastfeeding is always a better option. The expressed feed can be stored at room temperature for about four to six hours and can be refrigerated for two to three days. Indirect heating method is to be used to warm the refrigerated expressed breast milk. Ensure you sterilize all the parts of your pump before every use.

Nipple shield/nipple puller/nipple reformers may be used by mothers with flat nipples. Breast gel pads may be used by mothers with mastitis. If you face any difficulty in feeding, please consult your lactation expert without wasting any time.

Beneficial Food Items for Lactating Mothers

- 1–2 l sauf/ajwain/jeera water
- Coconut water
- Room temperature buttermilk
- Fresh soup
- Warm plain water
- Ginger/garlic
- Dates
- Nuts
- Apricots
- Peaches
- Jaggery
- Fennel
- Oats
- Flax seeds
- Eggs
- Paneer
- Room temperature curd
- Milk
- Chicken/fish
- Daal
- Fruits
- Salad

Dear Dad,

When it comes to breastfeeding a newborn, it is important for the entire family to encourage and support the new mother. Your baby can demand frequent feeds at night, which can become very exhausting for both of you as new parents. If needed, ask for help from your family members; share your night duties in waking up when the baby is up. The two of you together will be able to cater to your baby's need.

Love,

Dr Mahima Bakshi

4
Modern-Day Parenting the Traditional Way

As a new mother who stays busy taking care of her little one, you want to learn everything for your baby. You would get multiple advices, and not understanding which ones to follow, you would eventually end up reading about it on the Internet. Overwhelmed by the information there, you would hit the panic button. My advice here is to just follow what your baby's paediatrician says and trust your doctor. Every baby is different, so let the paediatrician decide what is right for your baby. To keep yourself happy, remember to stay calm.

It's good to listen to people. But when it comes to your baby, trust your instincts. You know what is best for them.

Gradually, you will understand the likes and dislikes of your baby and how to calm them down.

Now, the question arises: 'How does one stay calm? Is it so easy?' Well, you need to train your mind to stay calm when the baby cries or else you both will need your husband to babysit the two of you. Who would calm him down then? It should be understood that fathers too go through post-partum depression.

Seven-P Plan for Your Mental Well-Being

1. <u>Practise</u> relaxation: The more relaxed you are, the easier it is for you to stay calm when your baby gets fussy. So, take a deep breath when you need it the most. Relaxation techniques like breathing exercises, meditation and stretches would be healthy for you when done on a daily basis.
2. Increase <u>patience</u>: Remember, you have more responsibilities now. You cannot be venting out your anger or frustration on the baby, so learn to stay patient.
3. Set <u>parenting</u> goals: Define your goals as a new parent and discuss them with your partner. If you have clarity, it would be easier for you to achieve your goals.
4. <u>Partnership</u> as couple: Equal parenting is what we are heading towards, so ensure that your partner is

equally involved. Get them to read some books or attend parenting workshops to help them understand on how they can share responsibilities and not let you feel all by yourself in this new phase of your life.
5. <u>Playtime</u>: Playing with your baby can help you de-stress, so spend some playtime with your little one.
6. Call the <u>paediatrician:</u> If you are a step away from hitting the panic button and unable to decide whose advice to follow, consult your baby's paediatrician.
7. <u>Participate</u> in support groups: Meet other mothers with kids of your baby's age and interact with them, share how you feel and hear them talk. Support groups can be very helpful in ensuring you don't feel alone.

Let's give some thought to the traditional concept of 40 days. Spend the first 40 days learning how to participate in babycare activities and focus on recovering. Share what you learn in these 40 days with each other as a parent. Also, give your valuable time to your baby. These early days will never come back. Be it playing, bathing, narrating bedtime stories, do it all. They grow up too fast, but will always carry these memories in their heart, deriving their sense of emotional security.

Traditional Approach in Modern-Day Parenting

With everything now being modernized, many parents hire a *maalish waali* (masseuse) for giving massages to the baby. Many parents also choose to keep a full-time nanny to take care of the baby. While it is good to get a helping hand as you are new parents, it should be remembered that a baby does not need much from the two of you, but your touch, your voice, your smell, your care and your affection. So how do we ensure that your baby gets all of this?

Try taking care of the baby yourself. Be it about giving the baby a bath or burping them, you should do it. It should be your touch. If you are a new parent, learn how to look after the baby in the initial days from a nanny or a doctor, the latter being the best option.

Easy Parenting Tips

Modernization has impacted everything we know. Thanks to the twenty-first century, we have adapted to the western culture and lost touch with ours. I strongly believe that whatever our grandparents taught us must have been backed by some reasoning. And choosing what is best for your child from everything that you have been told and have learnt is the biggest challenge faced by modern parents. So, let me share some tips on modern-day parenting in a traditional way. I like to call it 'cocktail tips of parenting'.

Let's accept the fact that your baby was born by an equal contribution from both of you. The moment your baby is formed, your responsibility as a parent-to-be begins. Therefore, equal contribution of both parents should continue throughout the pregnancy and even after delivery. Once someone becomes a parent, they always remain one, even when the phases of parenthood change. So, I strongly believe in and promote equal parenting. We live in an era of gender equality and there is no space for the stereotypical thought of only mothers being the one who is involved in parenthood, taking up all the responsibilities by herself.

How Can the Partner Help?

- **Share responsibilities**: Talk it out. Divide work. A lot of times, men are expected to do certain things after becoming a new father—things they might have never done before. It would get easier for them if they were to be told how they could help. So talk to your partner about how you would want them to help you, being clear about the responsibilities you'd want to share.
- **Divide the night duty of looking after the baby**: Often, men feel that when the baby wakes up in the middle of the night, they are hungry and only need the mother. If men would be explained how they can help you with burping the baby or changing

diapers at night, they would understand their shared responsibilities better. Not every cry of the baby is a sign of them being hungry. Sometimes, they just need your company when they don't want to sleep.

- **Fathers can help put the baby to sleep:**
  It is not only the mothers who can put the baby to sleep. Fathers, too, need to learn the techniques. Babies love to be held close to the chest, hearing your heartbeat. So, fathers can do some skin-to-skin or practise the kangaroo mother care.

- **Fathers can help in burping the baby:**
  Anybody can help burp the baby. The baby needs to release the air that they tend to suck in while taking feeds. So, burping is as important as feeding. Apart from the mother, babies love the touch and voice of their fathers too. It can be a great way for the father and the baby to bond.

- **Fathers can help in changing diapers:**
  Who says that only women can change diapers? Help your partner learn how to change diapers and encourage them to practise doing it rather than telling them that they are doing it the wrong way. If the mother is not around and the baby has pooped, fathers should be able to step in instead of waiting for the caretaker to do it.

- **Fathers can take care of the new mother by showering some love, care and affection:**
  This is something that no one else but only the fathers can do. Smother her with hugs, kisses, cuddles and affection. Only you can help her feel like a queen with your attention; she would want to feel so more than anything else. Take care of her as she learns to take care of herself and the baby. Help her as she copes with the hormonal changes post delivery. Give her your attention the way you did during the pregnancy. Ask her how she feels and whether she had her meals; accompany her for appointments with the gynaecologist even after delivery the way you did during her pregnancy. Go with her and give your undivided attention to her and your baby. Be her support and keep telling her that she's doing a great job. Don't let her feel alone in this. Surprise her with small gestures, respect her choices and decisions and avoid forcing any rituals on her only because they are part of some traditions. Make her feel comfortable, give her the space to feed the baby and avoid having too many visitors when she wants to take her nap. Make her believe that she is as important as the baby.

Impact of Relationships

Now, let's get to the simplest way of parenting. We all have grown up watching our parents and most of us tend to get influenced by what we have seen—that can prove to be healthy or unhealthy. While some of us might have experienced very good parenting, some might have actually not had a good childhood due to a toxic environment at home—perhaps a disturbed marriage or financial crisis. And as we become parents, we many a time choose to follow a mix of some aspects of our traditional family culture and what we might like to change. Reading the following tips would help you understand what is it that your baby expects from you when it comes to parenting.

Current Situation

With the ambition of growing in one's career—which could be true for both partners—parenting has actually become more challenging over the years, more so if you live in a nuclear family. Many of us want to maintain a balance between work and home, and wish to have a strong support system and an understanding partner. If you are at home, you think of work, and if you are at work, you think of the baby. Many mothers start feeling guilty, as a result of which they are neither able to take care of the baby, nor concentrate on the work front.

What Can One Do?

Maternity Leave

Mothers need to plan their maternity leave sensibly. Avoid going on leave early in the pregnancy if things are going smooth. Understand about the maternity leave policy from your company HR. If possible, try to work till the last day of your pregnancy. Some mothers also choose to take a break from work to only focus on the baby. That is your choice. Discuss about it with your husband, so that he supports you in whatever you decide.

Paternity Leave

Fathers need to plan their leaves too. The mother needs the father to help her in the labour room and once she's back home. The baby needs him too, be it his touch, his voice or his warmth. He can try to make the early phase of transition easy for the wife and the baby by being available for them. He needs to be caring, empathetic and supportive. Many companies have different policies for paternity leave and give it as paid leaves. Some offer at least 14 days. Spending at least the first week to 10 days at home with her is recommended.

Waking Up at Night

Waking up at night becomes the most challenging thing to do as new parents for most couples. I have seen parents opting for supplement feeds—which takes time to digest and ensures the baby sleeps for four to six hours straight—at night so that they don't have to wake up in the middle of the night. Many fathers feel that their sleep gets disturbed when the mothers wake up every two to three hours to breastfeed the baby and turn on the lights or when the baby cries. Thus, they prefer to sleep in another room. This, again, is a very wrong practice that must be stopped.

The baby tends to get hungrier at night initially and sleeps more during the day. Both the partners should be able to take care of the baby at night. You can divide the night in two halves such that one of you gets to sleep for at least two to three hours at one go. If the baby needs to be breastfed, you can go back to sleep once you are done feeding them; the baby can also be breastfed in a side lying position, which would not need you to get up from bed. In case, the baby needs to be burped or is crying for a diaper change, then your husband can help so that you don't get to wake up every time the baby does at night. Your body makes more milk at night as that is the time when maximum lactation hormones are released. Thus, breastfeeding at night also reduces the chances of breast engorgement.

Quick Parenting Tips

- Ensure you spend quality time with your baby. Keep your phone aside.

Modern-Day Parenting the Traditional Way

- Try to keep the baby away from gadgets for at least the first five years.
- Take your child out for walks in a stroller.
- Play soft calming music for your baby.
- Talk to your baby even if they're too small to understand what you say.
- Arrange play dates for your baby with other babies of their age as they grow up and eventually start sitting on their own.
- Spend playtime with your baby.
- Avoid relying on your caretakers all the time for taking care of your baby.
- Take out time for your baby's daily activities, like giving them a massage or a bath.
- Take your baby for vaccinations on time—put up the dose chart on your fridge to remember.
- Baby-proof your house when needed. Generally, when the baby starts crawling around and tries to stand on their own, we know it's time to baby-proof everything.
- Try not to leave your baby unattended when they are awake.
- Avoid arguing or shouting at each other in front of the baby.
- Start learning how to change priorities.

Dear Mom,

You might get to hear about many traditional practices from the elderly in your family. Make sure you check with your baby's paediatrician once before following them blindly. Of course, you would not want to disrespect your elderly—the least you could do is hear them out. Before implementing what they advise, make sure to check with a doctor once to ensure that what you are doing for your baby has a scientific backing and will not prove to be harmful for them. Remember, at the end of the day we all want to ensure your baby's safety. While there might be many tips on baby care, only follow those which are beneficial for your little one.

Love,

Dr Mahima Bakshi

5
Preventing Post-Partum Depression

Post-partum depression can dampen a woman's happiness and excitement of becoming a new mother. Its severity can vary from case to case. It can also affect the way she takes care of her baby and can lead to worse consequences if not treated on time.

The first three months after delivery is just like another trimester in which the mother is in constant need of care, concern and affection. Most of the times, the family's attention gets shifted to the baby, overlooking the mother's needs. It should be understood that she is still undergoing physical and mental changes.

Happy Mommies, Happy Babies

We all must ensure that we constantly create awareness to help mothers identify post-partum depression on time. They should be able to talk about it comfortably. We need to break the stigma around a woman being depressed after becoming a mother.

As a woman delivers and enters motherhood, she experiences a lack of sleep and an outburst of emotions. She might experience maternity blues in the early days post delivery and that only goes away with time once the hormones settle down. However, if the feeling does not go away, then she should see an expert and get ruled out for post-partum depression.

Women who have been depressed in the past could be at higher risk of developing post-partum depression. Talking about it is very important to help her get over it. Most of the time, women feel that they will be judged if they reveal they have been suffering from post-partum depression. Thanks to the many celebrities coming out in public and talking about their depression journey, it has actually made a change in society. Communication is imperative for good mental health. Sadly, many of us, despite being surrounded by numerous people around us, hardly have anyone who would actually listen to us. This is the reason why many people end up suppressing their emotions.

New mothers can join support groups, where they can

get someone who would not only listen to them but also empathize with them, becoming a strong support system. If you are a new mother, follow these nine postnatal tips for good mental and physical health.

1. **Physical support**: Ask for as much physical support you need, be it for taking care of the baby or yourself or the household chores. If you have a joint family, you can discuss and make a plan in advance on who will be supporting you and how. If you have a nuclear family, you may choose to call over your mother or mother-in-law to stay with you for the first few weeks till the time you settle down. If no one, you could keep a caretaker, who has experience in taking care of babies and new mothers. Convenience and comfort are what you need.
2. **Appreciate yourself**: You should feel appreciated and be told that you are doing great. Every time you look at yourself in the mirror, please tell yourself that you are doing amazingly well as a new mother and that you would stay committed to your well-being and that of your baby no matter how hard it gets. Partners need to support their wife by constantly encouraging and reminding her that she is doing a great job.
3. **Some pampering**: Try giving incentives to yourself. Every time you add a pack of diapers to your cart, also buy something for yourself. This will boost your happy hormones.

4. **Good nutrition**: Give good attention to what you eat and don't go on living on mere daliya and khichdi. I have seen many families discouraging new mothers from drinking plain water, fearing it bloats the stomach. Instead, talk to your doctor, consult a good dietician and follow a healthy diet chart. I tell my patients to eat and enjoy everything to boost happy hormones as long as the food to be consumed is cooked at home, is fresh and not spicy. Of course, alcohol should be avoided.

5. **Avoid house arrest**: Many families follow the practice of not allowing the new mother to step out of the house for the first 40 days and only visits to the doctor is allowed. Talk to your partner and ask him to support you when it comes to you going to your parents' house or meeting friends for a quick tea or lunch. The two of you could also go to a nearby café for some change of scene. Of course, you should avoid going somewhere far or be away for long hours in the initial days as the body is still trying to adapt to the new sleep cycle and the new routines involving you and the baby.

6. **Don't hesitate in seeking help**: Many women suffer from post-partum depression. If you feel you are suffering from any symptoms of the same, then seek help from a professional at the right time. Let your doctor help you out.

7. **Postnatal exercises**: Take out time for your postnatal exercises. You doctor can teach you simple stretches, back exercises, neck exercises, leg exercises and shoulder curls with arms raises. They will not just help you maintain blood circulation but also correct your posture, prevent backache and boost the level of endorphins in the body, hence making you happy. Plus, it will also help in toning your body.
8. **Postnatal massages**: As your sleep cycle would get disturbed and you would have to adapt to your baby's sleep cycles, postnatal massages would act as a lifesaver. It would help your body and mind get relaxed, and make you feel lighter. Followed by a hot shower and a cup of chamomile tea would become your most favourite routine of the day and one that you would start looking forward to. You deserve this.
9. **Dress comfortably and wear colourful clothes**: Fill your wardrobe with clothes that allow you to easily nurse your baby. Don't shy away from wearing bright colours every now and then. Put on some make-up if you want to and take selfies with your baby.

Let every day be a celebration of motherhood. Make memories with your husband and your baby as you transition to the new phase of your life. Follow the nine tips for postnatal well-being after completing your nine months of pregnancy. These will not just boost your happy hormones but also help you stay in touch with your own self and not let you lose your individuality after you become a mother.

Every woman is different and, thus, every woman needs to be cared for differently post delivery. In some cases, the mood swings could continue for a while even after giving birth. Remember to take care of your health. If you will not be in good health, how would you take care of your baby.

Dear Dad,

Your partner would need a lot of emotional support during her post-partum phase. Her body and mind are going through many changes and taking care of the little one can become very exhausting at times. Nurture her, support her, take her out for movies or dinner dates just like you did earlier. Let her know that she is doing a great job. Appreciate everything she does to take care of your baby.

Love,

Dr Mahima Bakshi

6

Me Time

As you transition into the new phase of your life, you would be slowly trying to adapt to the changes that come with it.

While a woman's partner's support is imperative, I strongly believe that it is her 'me time' that acts as her best friend.

I strongly believe that a woman's perfect best friend is her me time. She gets so busy playing all the roles and fulfilling the responsibilities, that she hardly gets the time to understand what she feels, what she wants and who she really is. As the responsibilities grow, she tries to match up to the expectations of the people around her, pursue her career, manage her job and her household. Amidst all of this, she probably loses touch with her real identity. As she steps into motherhood, she slowly starts learning about her baby, simultaneously trying to figure out each day as it comes, wishing for a good sleep of eight to 10 hours without having to worry about waking up in the middle of the night to change diapers. Her mind needs some peace and rest. The question is: 'How can she learn to adapt to this new phase of her life without losing the woman she had been to the mother she has become?'

She needs constant support from her partner to be able to take out time for herself, unwavering understanding from her family that she might try her best to be perfect but there could be times when she can't and constant motivation from society that she should not lose her own real identity and self-worth.

Start investing in your me time right from your pregnancy. Your me time is for you to not lose touch with who you are. Continue to stay committed to yourself when it comes to having some me time, even after you give birth.

- Spare 40–60 minutes for yourself everyday. Ask your partner or family to take care of your baby—maybe when asleep—so that you can get those few minutes to yourself and indulge in things which are essential to you for your well-being.
- Keep your mobile phones away at that time. Unfortunately, as we head towards the future, our mobile phones would become our best friends

instead of our me time. Practise some mindfulness techniques in your me time instead of scrolling through your phone.

- Do some stretches to relax your mind and body. You can also do some chanting or just sit down quietly and meditate.
- Pursue any hobby of yours—painting, dancing, singing, cooking, gardening, etc.—for 20 minutes.
- Watch something that you like. It can be a movie, web series, documentary, anything. It would be better if you watch something on your TV instead of your smaller gadgets.
- Take a hot shower to relax yourself. You can use essential oils for adding some aroma while you take a shower and de-stress yourself during that time.
- A quick postnatal massage would also do wonders, relaxing your body and mind. You can call a masseuse or a postnatal massage therapist daily who can help relax your muscles with some great therapeutic postnatal massages. It will help boost your oxytocin levels along with your milk supply.
- Aromatherapy not only helps in inducing relaxation, but it also helps in changing the whole aura of the place. You can use some diffuser lamps, incense sticks, candles or aroma oils and do some aromatherapy for a while. Allow the therapy to rid

you of all the negative energies, and help you detox your mind and soul.

- Go out to meet your friends once or twice a week during your maternity leave or even later if you can. When you meet your friends, remember to talk about yourself and them, and not about the baby. I always tell my patients that sometimes when we meet other mothers of the same age group as ours, it's exciting to have them as a group support in the beginning, but later it only leads to conversations around the babies. Hence, hang out with friends with whom you can discuss different things. They could also be from a different age group.

- I always feel that nothing brings me closer to my soul better than penning down my emotions. So you can start maintaining a journal where you jot down the emotions and experiences you go through everyday. It would eventually help you realize how you feel and what you want, and help you get closer to your baby and your husband. It could even make you realize when you need to seek help, emotionally or physically. And, of course, pen down the memories of the moments you get to share with your baby. It could be turned into a baby journal too.

- Take pictures of yourself too rather than only taking those of your baby. Many new mothers end up filling their phone with thousands of pictures

every month, trying to capture every moment spent with their baby, only to realize later that their phone storage has outrun its capacity. Give yourself some importance too. Dress up, put a smile on your face and capture a picture of yourself too with the baby.
- You can plan weekend getaways with your partner and your baby. You can spare yourself an hour at the hotel and use the spa or the poolside to take a dip and relax to rediscover your inner goddess by coming closer to nature. Meanwhile, your partner can take care of the baby in the hotel.

Spending time with your parents and family is also a good option. New mothers, anyway, like visiting their mothers when it comes to spending some me time. But this should not mean that the entire responsibility of the newborn comes on the woman and her mother. Always encourage sharing of parental responsibilities.

Allow yourself to slowly sink into this new phase of your life. Walk towards embracing motherhood holding your partner's hand, ensuring that you walk towards parenthood together. Take support of your partner, encourage and allow them to be involved and share responsibilities, let them learn how to take care of the baby rather than depending upon the caretakers all the time. Amidst all of this, do not forget to find the time to take care of yourself—your me time. Self-love and self-worth will always keep you charged up to take care of your baby and yourself in the same manner.

Dear Mom,

As you embark on your new journey of parenthood, you need to also be who you were before becoming a mother. Do what you liked doing, take out time for yourself and keep giving yourself time to learn. You will gradually master everything and learn to strike a balance between giving time to yourself and your newborn. If need be, take help from your friends and family—no one is going to judge you. Do whatever it takes to make this transition easier for yourself. Celebrate your motherhood by celebrating your own self. Don't let go of your individual identity. You, too, are precious.

Love,

Dr Mahima Bakshi

7

Making Your Child Independent without Getting Detached

We all tend to get busy with our own lives. Most of the hours during the day are spent at work and whatever little time we are left with is mostly spent either in traffic or in completing our everyday chores at home. What lives would our kids lead when they grow up? From a very early age, they get busy with school tuitions, sports classes and homework. How much time do they get to spend with their parents once their school life begins?

It is only in the early years when the kids get to spend more time with their parents, learn from them and enjoy carefree moments instead of worrying about attending classes, completing homework or scoring in tests. While they are young, be sure to give them a sense of emotional security, and let them know they are loved and are not alone.

Lately, many parents have been trying to give gadgets to their child to keep them busy, so that they can complete their chores in the meantime. Doing so might lead the child to feel emotionally detached from the parents and get them hooked to using gadgets. This is something that needs to be fixed. The question is: 'How can we make the child independent from the very beginning and yet not detached from the parents; how can we make them feel loved, emotionally secure and let them know that their parents always have their back.' Build up that closeness with your baby from the very beginning. Develop a strong bond so that your child feels attached to you and can share all of their feelings with you comfortably as they grow up. Eventually, as the child gets comfortable with their parents and feels secure enough, they can be taught how to become independent too. Following are some tips you can follow as new parents right from the very beginning.

- Let your baby sleep in the same room as you.
- Be there for your baby when they cry. Remember, crying is their way to communicate what they need.
- Play with the baby. Involve yourself in their daily activities like massages, baths, etc.
- Talk to the baby more often even if they cannot understand yet. Remember, you used to talk to your

baby during the pregnancy. Your baby wants to hear your voice and seeks your attention.
- Look into their eyes when you talk. This would be your way of letting them know that you love giving your attention to them.
- Hold them close to your chest more often. One place where your little one would feel the most secure is your chest as they can hear your heart beating. Holding your baby close to your chest is also called the kangaroo mother care position. The father, too, can practise doing this.
- Don't get influenced by too many advices. Every parent is different and so is every child. Only follow what is good for your baby. When the need arises, take advice from your paediatrician. At times, you might also have to follow your instincts. Do what you think is right for the baby.
- Help them develop social skills. Take them out for walks in strollers, let them see new faces. Expose them to different objects and different colours.
- Try to ensure they spend time with their grandparents. Don't hesitate in handing over the baby to them as they too would want to show their love to the little one. If they don't stay nearby, then make it a point to travel once in a few months, so that your baby gets to bond with the grandparents too. It is healthy for the baby's growing phase.

- Get them some textured books to learn. These help in stimulating your baby's sense of touch and help in their neurological development. In the first five years, babies go through maximum neurological development and growth during which all five senses should be stimulated.
- Sing lullabies while putting them to sleep and read bedtime stories.
- Take them for play dates with kids of their age and let them learn how to interact with them as they grow up.
- Help them learn about sharing. Encourage them to show their toys to other babies and let them play.
- Give them some time with their toys so that they can do some imaginative playing and explore their toys.
- Play peek-a-boo. As your baby learns to sit, hide your face with a cloth and remove the cloth after a few seconds to show your face. You can also hide behind a sofa and then pop up to show yourself. Doing so will help your baby understand that their parents will come back even if they are away for a while.
- Hide their favourite toy and then show it to them after a while, so that they learn that even if their favourite things disappear for a while, they can be found again.
- Avoid distractions during their feeds. Do not give

them gadgets or switch on the TV during meals.
- Start letting them spend time with your family members while you are away, so that they learn to be without you for a while, knowing that you will come back. Start with leaving them in a separate room with another family member or a babysitter, while you are at home. Once they get comfortable with that person, start leaving them with the said person while you go away somewhere nearby.
- Before you plan to return to work, start training them to stay at home without you, happily looking forward to your return rather than being anxious and fussy until you come back.
- Try attending some mom and me or dad and me workshops organized by playschools, which help in preparing kids stay at daycares, away from their parents.
- As your child crosses six months and starts consuming complementary feed, encourage them to sit on a feeding chair with their own plate and spoon.
- Encourage your baby to drink using a sipper.
- Put your baby in a car seat whenever you take them out in a car.
- Read books on parenting to improve your knowledge on how to take care of your little one.

These small efforts during the early years of your baby's life can help in their growth and make them emotionally stronger. It would also help in preventing separation anxiety once you return to work or when you send them to playschool.

When Is the Right Time to Introduce Your Little One to Gadgets?

Due to Covid, we have become used to spending time in the virtual world instead of the real one. For many of us, online classes and work from home only made us spend more time on our gadgets, which definitely helped us stay connected with our jobs, family and friends, but got us so used to the virtual world that now if we have to imagine ourselves without our gadgets, we would struggle.

If we introduce our kids sooner to gadgets, they get hooked to the same early in life, and later we go on complaining that they do not spend any time with us. Parents, thus, need to control the duration their child spends on gadgets from the very beginning.

Introduce them to gadgets only after they have turned at least five or seven. You need not flaunt in front of your friends that your child already knows how to use an iPad or an iPhone by giving them one. Instead, keep them away from gadgets as much as possible.

But the question remains: 'What about us? Don't

kids follow observational learning at home? Don't they learn from watching what their parents do? So can we be hypocrites and not follow what we preach to our child and then expect them to do so?' Definitely not. So start with making changes in your own lifestyle. Try to reduce the time you spend in front of a screen, now that things have started getting better in the post-Covid world. Keep your phones away when there are friends and families sitting around you. Prefer face-to-face conversations instead of phone calls and text messages on social media to stay connected. Try to organize small dinners or get-togethers at home and invite friends and family to let your kids observe that real relationships have more value over reel connections.

Try to do some digital detox. You may decide to go off social media for some time or keep your phone aside. Prefer using a bigger screen over smaller ones and reduce your screen time by making conscious efforts.

Encourage your child to indulge in real activities instead of playing online games or getting hooked to PlayStation. Make a change in your lifestyle too. When you and your partner sit together once you are back from work, try to keep your phones aside and make a conscious effort in spending more valuable time with each other. Give your undivided attention to each other before your start figuring out how to do that for your child. Make the change now. It will be a healthy move.

Many studies prove that gadget or Internet addiction has become a threat to mental health and can lead to mental health issues.[3] Many hospitals have started de-addiction programmes to help people get rid of such addictions. Hence, the later you introduce your kids to gadgets, the better it is for their future. They all eventually learn it anyway without even being taught.

Make conscious efforts for all relationships in your life, be it with your parents, in-laws, partner, siblings or friends. Your kid will observe and learn what they see. Set a good example for them, so that they understand the importance of valuing relationships from the very beginning.

Dear Mom and Dad,

As you grow into parenthood, each and every thing you do would shape your baby's future. The initial five years play a very important role in your child's development. So try to follow things that would help your baby become emotionally secure, as the first five years form the future mental health of your baby. The more emotionally secure they feel, the easier it would

---

[3]Cash, Hilarie, et al., 'Internet Addiction: A Brief Summary of Research and Practice', *Current Psychiatry Reviews*, Vol. 8, No. 9, 2012, pp: 292–98; Das, Aswathy, et al., 'Technology Addiction among Treatment Seekers for Psychological Problems: Implication for Screening in Mental Health Setting', *Indian Journal of Psychological Medicine*, Vol. 39, No. 1, 2017, pp: 21–27.

be for them to become an independent child as they grow up. Spend quality time with your baby. These initial days would never come again, so cherish each day.

Love,

Dr Mahima Bakshi

8.

Playtime with Your Baby

Playing can be therapeutic in many ways. It makes the baby feel good, exercise their limbs and brain, and also helps in releasing happy hormones. It induces relaxation that helps the baby sleep better.

Now the question is: 'What are the different ways to ensure your little one finds new ways of playing and gets the maximum benefits out of the same?' Playing also offers many opportunities of learning.

This chapter talks about how you can play with your baby ensuring they get your time and attention.

Playing through Massages

Who says massages can only be given by grandparents or *maalish waalis*? Your baby gets the best massage when it is done by you. Your touch will create a magic for your baby that can't be replaced by any other. How can this massage be turned into a playtime with your baby? It doesn't have to be an oil massage; it could be a dry one, where your mere touch can relax your baby and help you bond with them.

Place your baby in front of you on the bed, table or crib. Avoid bending too low for the massages as your bad posture can lead to a backache. Try to keep the baby above your waist level the way it is advisable when changing their diapers. Start massaging from the shoulders and then go on to the wrists. Do this multiple times in a slow and relaxed manner without exerting too much pressure. For the lower body, start with the thighs, moving down towards the feet in a soft and slow circular motion.

To make it more fun for your baby, look into their eyes and talk to them while massaging their arms. You can also sing or play some nursery rhymes, poems or songs for them. You will see the baby respond with kicking their legs and smiling. You can massage the tummy, too, using the tip of your fingers—this also aids in baby's digestion. You can use almond, coconut or olive oil for giving massages. Remember to take in just a little amount of oil to moisturize your hands before the massage. Avoid massaging your baby with *malai* or milk cream as it may lead to skin reactions or baby acne.

Exercising Your Baby's Limbs

After the massage, work on stimulating your baby's limbs further. You can hold their hands and try moving their arms up and down, meanwhile doing some counting to make it interactive for the baby. Similarly, you can hold their ankles and move both their feet up, such that the knees move towards their chest. This movement also aids in the baby's digestion and helps in removing gas from their stomach. It will make them feel more relaxed. You can repeat these movements a couple of times. A month after their birth, you could start giving them some tummy time. Talk to your paediatrician to find out more about giving tummy time to your baby.

The process can be followed by a relaxing bath. Breastfeed the baby after the entire process, so that they get their feed and can sleep peacefully for a couple of hours. During this time, you could catch up on your sleep too, utilize that time to complete your household chores or spend some me time.

All this will not just help stimulate your baby's mind and body but also aid their digestion, increase their appetite and, hence, improve their growth and development.

Playing While Reading

Many parents wonder when is the right time to introduce their child to books. I advise them to start buying books to read out to their baby once they learn how to sit, observe, touch and feel. Buy some touch-and-feel books that can be used by the baby for feeling different textures. You can help your baby sit with a back support as you read out a book to them. They would love hearing you. You can try some voice modulation to catch their attention. Don't worry about them being able to understand the story, as it is more about introducing the concept.

In fact, I strongly advise pregnant women to read a lot. That's the best time to introduce your baby to books, be it through the womb. Textured picture books aid in tactile stimulation. Story time session is a great way to bond with your baby. You can start setting up your child's library by stocking it with picture books, texture books, bedtime storybooks and all the books you've read throughout your pregnancy. It will help inculcate reading habit in your baby.

Play with Paper, Pencil or Crayon

Once your baby learns how to sit, you may give them a crayon and a paper to scribble on. It will be good for the development of their motor skills and grasping reflex as they learn how to hold and scribble. It doesn't matter if they do not know how to draw or write yet. Once they learn how to hold the crayon and scribble on paper, it will stimulate their imagination and, thus, act as a brain exercise too. So to start with, get your baby to hold the big and thick crayons that are easier for them to hold. Gradually, once they learn how to hold and use the thick colours, you can try giving thinner ones, eventually introducing pencils or paint as they grow up. Ensure that the baby doesn't try putting any of it into their mouth.

Colour therapy can be very beneficial in relaxing your baby's mind and also help you unwind. Try and preserve all the art created by your little one—it would be nice to show them their creations once they grow up. Their little efforts and imagination are parts of their learning process.

Playing with Blocks

Playing with building blocks has been a childhood memory for all of us. We all have spent a lot of time, as kids, building the tallest tower until it falls down. Playing with blocks involves a lot of brain stimulation, motor skills and efficiency. Each time your baby picks up a block, they do so with a goal in mind. To be able to achieve the same would mean a great sense of happiness and achievement to them. You can introduce your baby to blocks after four to six months. They would love to try to pick up each block and feel a sense of achievement in simply holding it and showing it you. Let them learn how to play with it at their own pace.

Similarly, you can also introduce your baby to ring game wherein they have to hold a huge ring and put it on a stand such that the rings are stacked on top of one another. This is another great motor skill and coordination game for your baby that can be tried once they are able to sit.

Playing with Puzzles

Once your baby is older than eight to 10 months, they would probably start getting bored of their toys and start wanting to play with something new to explore their creativity. Jigsaw puzzles remain to be kids' favourite. You could start with the bigger-sized puzzle pieces, the ones that come in books, and let your baby try putting the pieces into the frame. Over a period of a few weeks, they would be able to complete the puzzle under your guidance. Eventually, you can give them puzzles with smaller pieces in it.

Playing with Clay Dough

Once your baby is over a year old, they would want to explore new activities instead of just playing with their regular toys. At this stage, you can introduce them to clay dough and help them make small figurines. It would help them learn about textures and also refine their motor skills and coordination. This is good for their brain stimulation. The baby gets a sense of achievement each time they're able to mould different shapes from that clay dough.

Playing Peek-a-Boo

Peek-a-boo is a great way of not just playing with your baby but also to letting them learn that every time you disappear, you will reappear right after. It's also a great way to make your child feel emotionally secure and not become clingy to you, so that when you start working or when the baby starts going to playschool, things don't get very challenging for them. The game has been discussed in the previous chapters too.

Please remember that when it comes to parenting, it is important to help your child learn in a fun-filled way instead of waiting for them to grow up and learn to recite alphabet in front of your guests. Playtime activities are very effective and strong learning methods for your baby. It also offers you the chance to take a break from your responsibilities and simply spend some time with your child, recollecting your own childhood days. Your presence in their playtime is what they seek as babies. Your child's learning begins right from the early days where your (both the parents') contribution makes a huge impact on their growth. So take out time to sit down with your baby and play with them.

Dear Dad,

Playing with your little one is a great way for you to bond with your baby. Engage with your baby using the various ways mentioned in the chapter. Arrange play dates for your little one with kids of your colleagues/friends. Put extra effort to ensure that your baby is able to play with different people. This would help in building up their social skills. If possible, try to get a pet, who could be your baby's companion.

Love,

Dr Mahima Bakshi

9

Getting Back in Shape

Many women look at their wardrobe and dream of fitting into the clothes they wore before their pregnancy. While many do make it happen, there are also those who are not able to get back in shape. Promise yourself that you would do everything it takes to regain your pre-pregnancy shape soon. Don't try becoming a superwoman to be able to do that. Take it slow and steady. You need not hurry.

So how much weight gain is good and how can one shed off those pregnancy kilos are the questions that every new mother has. Let's get into the depth of it so that you can understand your body and work on it accordingly.

So mothers, do remember that every pregnancy is

different and so is every body. Ideally, the pregnancy weight gain should be slow and steady, and one needs to avoid sudden excess weight gain. Weight gain post delivery is definitely a big no. So, keep a check on it. There is no standard pregnancy weight gain range. However, if one has a normal Body Mass Index (BMI), then one should ideally be gaining within 10–12 kg. Avoid gaining over 15 kg. However, if one is already overweight, then it's better for one to lose some kilos before planning a pregnancy. Ideal weight gain that can be achieved in three phases.

1. Pre-Conception Phase

Get your BMI checked once you decide to plan a pregnancy. If you are overweight, work hard on losing some kilos. Losing weight, whether you are overweight or obese, will help improve your fertility. It is also beneficial for those who have Polycystic Ovary Syndrome. You would also be able to prevent gestational diabetes or hypertension in your pregnancy. So give yourself at least three months before conceiving and focus on your body by working on your BMI and improving your lifestyle so that your body is better prepared for the pregnancy changes. In case of being underweight, try improving your diet to gain some weight. That would be needed for better growth of your baby in your womb.

2. Post-Conception Phase

Once you have received those two lines on the test, your pregnancy journey begins. Your body would go through various hormonal changes. Some women experience such excessive nausea in the first trimester that they sometimes end up losing weight. However, once you start gaining weight, try to ensure that your weight gain is as gradual as possible. How can that be ensured? Maintain a healthy lifestyle.

Watch what you eat: Avoid processed foods, carbonated drinks, fried foods or packaged foods and juices. Prefer home-cooked food and consume lots of fruits and vegetables. Include lean proteins in your diet. Stay hydrated.

Stay active: Maintain a healthy and an active lifestyle instead of following a sedentary one. Make a physical fitness routine and do pregnancy exercises. Prenatal workouts are necessary for every pregnant woman to avoid gestational diabetes and hypertension. It also helps in preventing sudden excess weight gain. So, talk to your obstetrician and consult a prenatal fitness expert who can guide you with some pregnancy exercises. You can also refer to my previous book, *Birthing Naturally*,[4] which includes some great prenatal workout pictures to help pregnant women

---

[4]Bakshi, Dr Mahima, *Birthing Naturally,* Penguin eBury Press, 2018.

stay fit and healthy. I generally advise pregnant women to do prenatal workouts for at least an hour thrice a week and walk daily for 30 minutes. It also helps in preparing the body for optimum foetal positioning and natural childbirth.

3. Post-Delivery Phase

Once you deliver, you are surrounded with the joy of welcoming a new life and your world starts revolving around your baby. You would lose some kilos in the form of baby weight and the placenta would be taken out. Looking at your belly, you might still feel pregnant, but remember that your uterus will take time to shrink back to how it was before the pregnancy. The fluid retention goes away gradually. What are the most important things that a new mother should keep in mind to make it easy for her to naturally lose her pregnancy weight?

Diet

- Go natural for the first 40 days. Eat home-cooked fresh food with some portion of daal, vegetables, multigrain roti and yoghurt salad for lunch and dinner. Add some fish or chicken too if you can or add egg and cereals to breakfast. Addition of nuts and seeds to your diet will also be beneficial.
- Avoid lactation laddoos. Prefer to make some lactation homemade mixture (popularly known as

panjeeri) with jaggery and add raagi and coconut in it instead of wheat.
- Saunf ajwain jeera water not only helps in better lactation but is also a great detoxifying agent for the new mother. So try to have around 1–2 l of it daily for the first six months for weight loss. Apart from that, have other liquids too—regular water, coconut water, fresh juices, buttermilk, soups, milk, etc., should be consumed daily. Don't go on a diet for weight loss too soon. Consume healthy foods that would help you in better lactation.
- Talk to your doctor about continuing iron and calcium supplements post delivery to prevent deficiency of the same.

Breastfeeding

Many moms don't realize that breastfeeding is beneficial for the mother's body too. Breastfeeding makes a mother burn calories and also helps in uterus involution making the belly shrink. So no matter how tiring you think it could get, keep breastfeeding your little one for the first six months exclusively and notice its positive effects on your body. You will undergo some amazing weight loss.

Postnatal Exercises

Many moms don't know when and what exercises to do post delivery. You can start with simple postnatal exercises from the second day of your delivery itself. Consult a physiotherapist for that. Simple exercises like ankle-toe movements, knee bending and stretching, thigh squeezes with a pillow in a lying position, bridging, back isometrics, shoulder rolls, arm raises and posture correction in bed must be done. I generally advise new mothers to do these basic exercises after every feed as it helps in not just improving blood circulation and posture post delivery but also in preventing backache. They could also walk for 15–20 minutes with breaks in between, if needed. One can wear a postnatal binder belt after consulting a gynaecologist as it makes it easier to walk around with an abdomen support.

After four weeks of natural delivery and six to eight weeks of C-section, you can start doing some more postnatal workouts. Get checked for diastasis recti before you indulge in core workouts. As the abdominal muscles get stretched in pregnancy, many women end up with diastasis recti. Our abdominal muscle set (core muscles) are made of left abdominal and right abdominal set of muscles. Diastasis recti is a condition in which there is a gap between the two set of muscles. It can lead to pelvic floor dysfunction, backache, urinary incontinence, etc. It generally closes on its own in four to six weeks' time. It's always good to get yourself checked by a physiotherapist before starting any heavy workout or gymming. In case, the gap has not closed yet, consult your physiotherapist on what exercises should be done to close the gap. Till then, only continue with strengthening exercises, and that too, without heavy weights. Light running, jogging or postnatal yoga workouts can be initiated.

I advise moms to continue wearing their maternity pants while doing postnatal exercises as it keeps the core supported during the exercises and helps maintain core strength for faster healing and weight loss.

Once the muscle strength improves, start the toning workout to reduce inches and prevent skin sagging as you start losing weight. Remember, just like we wanted gradual weight gain in pregnancy, we also want the weight loss to be gradual to avoid skin sagging. You may add 30 minutes of cardio workouts gradually and increase your intensity of training with time. You can consult a dietician to help you with a weight-loss diet plan as you start your heavy workouts while continuing with the breastfeeding ensuring that your lactation supply doesn't get affected. The quality of your breast milk also depends a lot on what you eat. So avoid going on crash diets or any fad diets. Just keep it simple with a lot of healthy food items and eat on time.

Postnatal Massages

Don't we all love massages? I think it's the best way to get pampered, especially for a new mother who has been on her toes taking care of the baby, going through sleepless nights. Massages would help relax her body and give some rest to her mind. But do you know that massages also help in improving blood circulation and in toning of the body, such that the new mother can achieve better weight loss results. Many families follow a tradition wherein the woman must get postnatal massages for the first 40 days post delivery. I often ask them, 'Why stop at 40 days? Continue with the massages even after that.' So try to get massages for at least two to three times a week so that your body can get rest post workouts. Plan a good postnatal workout and massage routine. Postnatal massages boost oxytocin levels, which in turn help in better release of milk. If you have undergone a C-section, wait for your gynaecologist to tell you when to start your tummy massages. Till then, enjoy upper body and lower body massages without touching the core, allowing your stitches to heal.

Stay Motivated

While many mothers wish to get back their pre-pregnancy body, only a few are able to. To stay motivated on your weight loss journey post pregnancy, don't lose hope and don't expect magic. Keep it slow. Don't throw your pre-pregnancy clothes right away. Set realistic goals with your trainer and give yourself a target. I generally give a target to my patients to get back to their pre-pregnancy shape by the first birthday of her baby. If you gain weight in the nine months of your pregnancy, you should also be able to lose the same and get a toned body in another nine months. Leaving aside the first three months post delivery, if a new mother starts doing her regular workouts and training starting from the fourth month onwards, she should be able to lose her pregnancy weight. Hence, work hard for those nine months during your postnatal phase and stay focused on achieving your goals until the first birthday of your baby.

Every body is different, so please try to learn what suits your body and what kind of workouts and diet your body responds to better. Please do not try to replicate somebody else's plan, try to get a customized plan for yourself with a good postnatal wellness expert who helps you achieve your weight loss goal in the healthiest manner, without letting your breastfeeding experience get affected.

Dear Mom,

Every new mother wonders when would she be able to fit into her pre-pregnancy clothes. Allow yourself a practical timeline. Don't give up. Follow a healthy lifestyle to shed off those extra kilos. Keep following your fitness regime while you take care of your baby. You might feel that you are multi-tasking, but all those efforts will not go to waste. You would gradually see the results and thank yourself for sticking to your determination. So remember the thumb rule: go slow, but go healthy!

Love,

Dr Mahima Bakshi

10

Complementary Feed

Once your baby crosses six months, only breast milk will not be sufficient to meet their nutritional demands. So the paediatrician would advise you to start giving them complementary feeds. Note that babies do not instantly consume everything you introduce them to. Hence, you will have to try different ways and stay patient.

How to Start

Start with appropriate positioning. If you make your baby sit in your lap and try spoon-feeding them, they might just want to get off your lap as a result of feeling trapped. So get a feeding chair for them. Seat them next to you in their feeding chair whenever you are having your meal. They will watch you eat and learn how to. You can start this exercise exactly a few days before you introduce them to complementary feed.

Get them a baby spoon and an attractive plate with brightly coloured pictures on it. The baby would feel they have their own eating space and independence. Put the food in their plate—they would touch the food and try to play with it holding their spoon. Let them do so as it is their way of accepting the food on their plate. Let them spend a few minutes with the food before you start feeding them using their own plate and spoon.

Remember to begin with a lot of patience. They might refuse to eat in the early few days and would only gradually get used to the taste and flavour. Keep trying for a while. Start with liquids like cereals and daal water as these are easier for the baby to accept. Apple purée and papaya purée can also be given. Start with 1–2 teaspoons and gradually increase it when your baby starts accepting the feed. Allow your baby a week's time for this. Initially, they spit out the solid foods, which is called the early rejection phase. You must also introduce them to water.

By the second week, you should be able to offer foods like porridge, blended khichdi, mashed sweet potatoes, mashed banana, raagi or sooji kheer to ensure your baby is consuming calorie-dense food. These will help them stay nourished. Steamed vegetables can also be given—they act as good sources of fibre.

Quantity and Frequency of the Foods for Babies

6–8 Months

Give 4–8 spoons of porridge or sooji kheer/khichdi 2–3 times a day.

8–10 Months

Give a quarter of a small bowl of porridge or sooji kheer/khichdi 2-3 times a day with an additional snack, like a finger food or mashed banana/sweet potato. Babies enjoy finger foods like steamed broccoli, baby carrot, baby corn.

10–12 Months

Babies can be given about half a bowl of porridge/kheer/khichdi or almost one small roti with daal for 2–3 times a day with a snack or two. It is okay for the baby to eat roti with daal after they turn about 10 months old, as the gums start becoming harder around this time.

Many babies refuse to consume the complementary feed directly. Try breastfeeding the baby for about five to seven minutes before giving them food. You can try giving it to them when they tend to get the hungriest and when your supply reduces—maybe towards the second half of the day.

Avoid giving them the complementary feed when they are fussy. The baby can get cranky when they have not slept enough, need a diaper change or when they are gassy. They might be hungry when they put their hand into their mouth. Look out for such signs before giving complementary feed to your baby.

What to Give

After starting with liquid food, you can move on to giving mashed banana, mashed sweet potato, which are loved by babies. Also give porridge (made of oats or raagi or blended khichdi). Gradually, add mashed vegetables like steamed carrots or steamed peas. Including different textures and flavours help in gradually letting the baby adapt to different types of foods.

Babies also enjoy raagi kheer and sooji kheer. One food item should be introduced at a time with the second one not being introduced before five to seven days. Observe any change in the baby during that time. In case of any change in stool pattern or skin rashes or breathing, talk to your doctor to rule out any food allergies that might have cropped up. Once your baby starts accepting solid foods around the eighth or ninth month, you can start giving them some steamed chicken or egg yolk. Avoid giving honey, cow milk, peanut and egg white for one year.

Talk to the paediatrician about the foods that can be

safely given to your baby and follow what is told to you. Avoid listening to others—every baby is different. No other liquid barring the breast milk should be given to the baby for the first six months. Encourage usage of feeding cups or sippers that can be held by the baby while sitting. Put a bib around their neck while feeding them meals. Not only does it keep their clothes clean but also helps them eventually establish that it is their meal time.

Avoid giving mobile phones to your baby to distract them while eating. Increase your patience level, if need be, to keep yourself from shouting at your baby if they refuse to eat easily. Do not give packaged foods to your baby, instead make home-cooked fresh food. Remember, any food that is fresh and prepared at home is better for your little one in comparison to the the food that is packaged and contains preservatives.

Breastfeeds Should Be Continued

Breastmilk contains immunoglobulins that helps develop your baby's immunity. You must continue breastfeeding your baby so that their gut health is maintained, giving them the immunity to fight any infection they might get exposed to while being introduced to solid foods. You might experience a drop in the frequency of breastfeeding as your baby would start feeling fuller with other foods. Try not to fill their tummy with too many fruit juices as that might suppress their demand for breastmilk. Continuing breastfeeding also helps in preventing constipation in babies.

If you are a working mom and have to return to work after six months, then you should start expressing milk to stock up for your baby. Try to breastfeed at night and before leaving for work. Leave behind the expressed milk, which can be given by someone else to the baby using feeding cups (avoid bottles). Express once or twice at work depending upon when your breast starts feeling fuller and heavier. Store the milk in a fridge or in an icebox in your office and bring it back home, so that it can be used for the next day for the baby in your absence. Once you are back home, try to breastfeed your baby. Try to give the evening meal to your baby yourself so that they get to bond with you.

Please note that while teething, your baby might get fussy—chewing on frozen baby carrots would help them relax their gums.

Daddy's Time with the Baby

Encourage your partner to give Sunday meals to your baby or on weekends if he reaches home before you. This would help in strengthening the bond between the two.

Fathers can be a huge help when it comes to feeding solids to your little one. Remember a lot of patience is needed and practice is what will help them master it. If not possible on other days, you can let your partner try feeding the baby on Sundays.

Dear Mom,

Postnatal phase is not just about nurturing your little one but also taking your time to thank your body for supporting you during pregnancy by doing your postnatal exercises that will help you stay fit and strong. It is also about thanking your mind to help you manage through the emotional changes by meditating to boost release of happy hormones. It is also about thanking your breast for providing nutrition to your baby through breast milk by eating right and healthy. Support yourself throughout the postnatal phase by taking naps, by getting massages and by taking out me time for yourself. Let others nurture you while you nurture your baby by being a part of support groups for new mothers. Commitment to take care of yourself will help you take care of your baby. You are as important as your newborn. Don't let your own well-being get neglected. Make the transitions easier for yourself by taking care of yourself in the right way. I know it is quite demanding and tiring. You are doing your best and you are amazing. Keep giving your best to nurture your baby and yourself with these amazing tips shared in the book.

Love,

Dr Mahima Bakshi

11

Impact of Couple's Relationship on the Baby

When a woman is pregnant, her husband is told to stay prepared to deal with the mood swings she would undergo as a result of the hormonal changes in her body. Well, we must also tell them that the hormonal changes do not end the moment the baby is born. They pretty much continue for several months, even after delivery. It might be a result of issues faced during breastfeeding, sleepless nights, the child being colicky, stretchmarks, changed body shape, etc. All these factors can add to the existing hormonal changes and that in turn cause the mood swings to persist. It might be worsened by post-partum blues in the initial few days and can also lead to higher chances of developing postnatal anxiety or depression.

Many a time if the couple does not have clearly defined roles and have not decided on how they plan to share those responsibilities, it can lead to heated arguments amongst them. Fathers need to get prepared to take care of the newborn, who might get fussy from time to time, and the mother, who might experience continued mood swings.

A lot of times, I feel that men are not given a 'heads-up' about what to expect from their wife post delivery. The reality does not match with what they had thought it would be and this gives rise to heated arguments, making it quite unhealthy for the relationship of the two.

Once their wife gives birth, most men think, 'I would finally be able to get some attention and not bear with the mood swings and emotional outbursts.'

Most women after having a baby think, 'I will get emotional and physical support from my husband. He will help me take care of the baby. He will wake up at night with me, he won't let me feel like I am alone in this and that only my life has changed. His priorities, too, will change.'

These different set of expectations from both the partners lead to arguments and relationship issues—something which nobody prepares them for.

Many husbands, in some cases, start sleeping in a separate room citing that they have to go to work the next day and thus need proper sleep. In many cases, husbands decide to leave the wife and newborn at his in-law's place thinking that she would get better care there instead of convincing his family to help his wife or do so himself. Why would the wife and the newborn want to be sent away? They would definitely want to be with the father as the baby would need to bond with both the parents.

The husband, as reiterated before, need to take care of his wife after she has delivered the baby just the way he did while she was pregnant. The post-partum period is quite delicate for the new mother as she is emotionally vulnerable during this phase—she doesn't want to feel that it is only her body or her life that must go through the changes while her partner can enjoy his same old life he lived before the baby was born. It can also get quite tiring for her with the sleepless nights and frequents feeds. She needs to be told by her partner that she's doing well and that he's proud of her. Support her while she transitions to the new phase of her life and let her know that she's not alone.

The new father needs to be told about what his wife and newborn expect from him; the wife, too, needs to tell the husband what he can do to help. Communication is the strongest tool that would help new parents transition into parenthood, not letting their relationship get impacted negatively. It can help them become more empathetic towards each other during the early days of parenthood, be more loving and affectionate towards each other as well as the baby. Men, too, develop post-partum depression. They, too, need to be told that they are doing well. They also need to be asked about how they are coping. They also need to be shown some love and affection for bearing all the mood swings of their wife.

Tips for New Parents on Equal Parenting

- As you enter your third trimester or after you get back from the hospital carrying your newborn in your arms, discuss with each other about your expectations and how the responsibilities are going to be shared. Attending couple classes during pregnancy helps too. Try to be together and help each other—remember that your baby hopes and expects you to provide them with a loving and caring environment, where you love and care for each other too.
- Surprise her with something special to make her feel valued about bringing another life into your life. It is popularly known as 'push present' in western countries. Irrespective of whether she delivered the baby naturally or underwent a C-section, gift her something special to make her feel so. It will also make your bond stronger and make her feel that you care for her. While others might be showering her with gifts, it would be your gesture, no matter how big or small, that would really help her overcome the birth trauma, if she faced any.

- Take some time off the baby too. While someone could babysit your little one at home after the breastfeeds, you both could step out for a drive or go to a nearby café to sit and talk for a while. Try to recall your pregnancy journey, try reminiscing about your days as newlyweds. Ask each other about how they feel about being a new parent. Appreciate each other and let your partner express their emotions—be it happiness, sadness, anger or love. Giving vent to every emotion is very important, so help your partner do that.
- Celebrate parenthood together. Remember that celebrations boost happy hormones. While you must be getting many visitors and family members at your home to congratulate you both, the two of you need to celebrate the arrival of your bundle of joy together.
- Show care, concern, empathy and love for each other. Spend some 'we time' at nights cuddling and kissing each other. This would help release oxytocin, the happy hormone. This would also minimize the chances of post-partum depression in both the partners. Resume your sex life once your wife is physically and emotionally prepared for it. Until then, make her feel attractive and beautiful, and make her fall in love with her body once again.
- Keep your gadgets away once you are back home.

Remember it is the quality time that you spend with your wife and your newborn that matters and not how much time you spend with them.
- After four to six weeks post delivery, you can plan a weekend getaway along with your little one—the three of you can go to a nearby resort to spend a weekend together. It would help you all get some break from your routine.
- Seek help from a counsellor if you feel that you are not able to cope with the changes. Don't take your relationship with your partner for granted. It's okay to seek counselling to be able to communicate better with each other instead of letting the relationship get adversely affected.

Dear couple/new parents,

Keep expressing your love for each other in small gestures. Don't let the spark die once you become parents. Talk to each other with respect and love. Avoid arguments and fights in front of your baby. Surround your baby with love and positive energy to let them feel protected around you. Give the best parenting to your little one right from the beginning, which is also inclusive of the pregnancy phase. Your baby can pick up all the energies you create around them, even when inside the womb. Love and care for each other, be empathetic towards each other and also help each other through the transition phase. Help your baby feel that you would care for them the way you care for each other. Welcome the little one into your world with happiness and joy.

Love,

Dr Mahima Bakshi

12

Working Parents

While many working parents find it difficult to find a babysitter, especially when they live in a nuclear family, some enjoy the perks of living in a joint family and are able to easily find a caretaker to look after their baby in their absence after they resume work. But to what extent is it okay to leave the baby with a caretaker. It should be you from whom your baby gets to learn. Also, would installing CCTV cameras inside the house be enough to ensure that your child is in safe hands in your absence?

Working mothers find it very challenging to leave for work after their maternity leaves are over. They have many apprehensions—how would the baby be given their complementary feeds, who will feed the baby in their absence, how would she manage breastfeeds, what if the baby needs her, what if she is not able to manage both work and home, what if the caretaker can't manage on their own, etc. Honestly speaking, it is not easy. Well, if there is sufficient family support, working parents can start training the baby to spend time with grandparents. So what would be the best option for working parents?

If you are planning to leave your little one with a caretaker and the grandparents are around, ask them to ensure that the baby is looked after well by the former. If this is not an option for you, then check with the organization you work at or your partner's company to see if they have a day-care option within the office campus or somewhere nearby, so that either you or your partner can go visit your baby, at least once or twice during the day. If even this is not feasible, then you can probably consider keeping a caretaker while leaving the baby at a day-care. Doing so, you would be leaving behind your baby with the caretaker under the day-care's supervision. Being at the day-care would also help your baby learn productive things.

Many mothers can also try talking to their company for being allowed the option of working from home for the next few months. It was due to Covid that many organizations realized that working from home is possible for new mothers and imperative when they do not have day-care facility to offer in their office premises.

With work from home option, mothers, too, can also supervise the caretaker while they look after the baby. This would allow her to manage her work better.

Fathers, too, can consider working from home so that the caretaker can look after the baby under his supervision. Both the parents should prioritize the baby equally. Having an open discussion with new fathers would help them become more sensitized towards taking care of the baby.

Now, there might be some cases where none of the available options are doable for the new mother. Under such a situation, I suggest to prioritize your baby for the first three years at least, as it is needed to shape the personality of your child. It is not only the mothers who should think about taking a break from work, men too should rise to the occasion. I have seen many husbands support their wives if the latter's career is at a peak and a career break is not advisable. By the end, it is a mutual call and the couple needs to collectively decide what needs to be done.

Many working mothers, who decide to go on a career break these days, become bloggers, influencers or even mumpreneurs. I have seen many women switch to a different career option and explore other business opportunities to be able to give more attention to their baby at home. Many fathers do that too—they start their own companies to be able to spend more time with their baby back home. These are some parenting choices the parents can make keeping in mind that their child needs them the most during the early years of their life.

Raising a child needs money and, hence, it is important for the parents to consider what kind of financial back-up they have even if one of them decides to take a career break or switch jobs. It is up to the parents to decide how they want to raise their child—whether both of them need to continue working or one can afford to go on a career break. If none of the two are workable, they might rely on grandparents' help, day-care facility in office campus or avail the option of work from home.

I have noticed that six months paid maternity leave option in our country has served as the biggest benefit for new mothers. It is a great step towards empowering women and uplifting their status in our country. Many countries are yet to offer such an extensive paid leave, so let's be grateful towards our country. Some companies also offer unpaid maternity leave. If nothing else seems to work out for you and your partner, you may ask for a sabbatical from your company, so that you can settle down with your baby and explore more options of managing your schedule with the new one.

How to Ensure Better Involvement of Working Dads

Starting from the time you begin trying to conceive, both partners should be equally encouraged to make lifestyle changes for the benefit of the baby.

During pregnancy, husbands should learn to manage their time better, so that they are able to accompany their partners for scans and visits to gynaecologists instead of sending them alone.

When it comes to childbirth, both should be equally involved in making lifestyle changes and preparing for the arrival of the baby. Husbands should attend classes and prepare themselves to assist their wives in the labour process.

Post delivery, the fathers must take a paternity leave and be part of the early transition phase where they share responsibilities of looking after the baby and also take care of the new mother instead of leaving behind the two with parents or caretakers. Many organizations do allow a paid paternity leave of two to four weeks. Talk to your company and find out about the paternity leave policy. Even if you are a businessman, do not rush into getting back to work. Your business cannot be more important than your newborn. Learn to change priorities and make choices. A father needs to learn to make gradual changes when it comes to making a priority shift. As a community, we all need to encourage men to make that shift and change the whole parenting system. This would help babies become emotionally healthier and happier as they would be able to get the best of everything from both the parents. There are many ways through which new fathers can work on equal parenting.

- Be empathetic towards your wife when she has to return to office once her maternity leave is over.
- Offer her help with other household activities when the helper is not around—don't let her feel overburdened with work.
- Offer help in feeding expressed breast milk to the baby. Bathe the baby when she can't. Offer to cook something for her to give her a break from kitchen chores.
- Help her emotionally, so that she does not slip into post-partum depression. Tell her she's doing a great job; push her to enjoy her me time and take her out for a staycation on weekends; surprise her with gifts; invite her friends over.
- Ask her about how her day was once you come back home from office or she does. Offer to take care of the baby once you reach home. Be involved in feeding the baby when you come back from work.
- If the baby wakes up in the middle of the night, wake up to check on them. Help in burping the baby and changing their diapers at night. It should not be only her whose sleep gets compromised.
- If the baby is unwell, offer to take an off from office, rather than always expecting her to do so. Be equally involved in taking care of the baby.
- Offer to babysit on weekends if you are not able to do so on weekdays.

- Let her know that it is not her life alone that has changed, and do so by taking responsibility of the baby.

How Working Moms Can Help Themselves

As much as we need our partner's support, we also need to become our own support system. This needs to be done to help yourself transition into motherhood. No one else but you can help yourself the most.

- Talk to your company HR to find out about the maternity benefits that they offer.
- Talk to your boss and explain your circumstances. Let them come up with solutions to help you.
- Once your paid maternity leave gets over, find out about leave extension, if needed.
- Start preparing your baby, such that they are able to spend some time apart from you without creating a fuss.
- Explore the option of work from home and talk to your boss about it. Discuss with your partner to see whether their company allows them to work from home if yours does not.
- Find out about the day-care facility within your office premises.
- Talk to your in-laws/parents to see whether they can come over to take care of the baby (with the

assistance of a caretaker).
- If none of the options are workable, discuss with your partner about taking a career break or taking up a job that allows you time to look after the baby.

Simply providing financial support to your child while they are growing up is not enough. They need more than that from you. They want to learn from you and want your time; they want to be surrounded by the love and respect that their parents have for each other. If becoming a mother is a beautiful thing, then so is becoming a father. Both need to make a priority shift keeping the baby in mind.

Women should not let their ambitions die once they become mothers. Continue achieving your goals. As you transition towards motherhood, be in touch with the woman you were and adapt to the woman you are becoming. Be the empowered mother of today. Give your partner the opportunity to help you, involve him in your decisions, in your pregnancy—let him feel equally involved. Sensitize him towards equal parenting right from the very beginning and help him realize the father he wants to be. Respect each other's careers, ambitions and time. Together, you both can sail through the journey of parenthood, letting your baby get the best of your time.

Dear Dad,

Your support can really work like magic for your partner, who has just become a new mother. Your care and concern can help her feel that she's not alone. You can help her through her postpartum depression, you can share responsibilities and help her physically so that she feels less exhausted. Your encouragement to let her live her ambitions and goals can make her feel more empowered. Your support is what she would always seek to raise the baby in the best way. Let us promote equal parenting together—the pregnancy could not have been possible without you and neither can raising the baby be. You play an important role for the new mother and the newborn. Your time, attention, care, affection and support is what they both need the most. So try to share responsibilities with her and let her know that she's not alone in this.

Love,

Dr Mahima Bakshi

13

Be the Baby

After having a baby, a new father generally wonders when would they ever be pampered by their wife again. They, too, like being looked after and taken care of. Don't we all want to be treated like a child sometimes despite being grown-ups? Even the new mothers, at times, want to take a break from babysitting and be looked after like a child by her husband.

I strongly believe that we all have a child inside us, who probably gets burdened and overshadowed by the responsibilities that we have to attend to as grown-ups. How would it feel if we allow that inner child to resurface sometimes even after we grow as parents? If given a chance, wouldn't we want to sleep like a child without having to worry about the baby's feed at night or without having to wake up when they cry? Wouldn't it be nice to be able to watch TV the entire day without having to worry about cooking or doing other household chores?

We all would love that. Even as you grow as a parent, learn to let yourself lose sometimes and let your partner do the same—it could be simple things like sleeping or watching a movie without getting disturbed. It's okay to be messy with your child as you play with them—we don't have to be perfect all the time. You can sit down and watch cartoons with your baby or play games with them that you yourself enjoyed playing once. You can also try hand painting with them. Once they grow up a little, teach them how to ride a bicycle and soon you'll be able to enjoy cycling around together with your child. Letting your inner child out sometimes will help in making parenting more fun.

Equal parenting becomes more interesting when you try to make parenting fun for each other and also respect each other's space and time. You could celebrate each other's birthday just like you would plan it for your kid. Shower each other with surprises and see the childlike happiness of your partner. This can also help in keeping the spark alive in your relationship after you have a baby.

So, my advice to the new parents would be to allow yourself and your partner feel like a child sometimes, ensuring that your baby is taken care of equally by the both of you. While you let your partner let themselves lose, you could take care of the baby, and vice-versa. The understanding and communication in your relationship is what would help you grow and embrace your role in equal parenting. Discuss with each other what you enjoyed doing when you were little and help each other rediscover the child that we all have within us.

Revisit your childhood memories when the two of you go out for a coffee date. You may also try to talk to each other's parents to find out more about your partner's childhood so that you can help them feel like a child again. Offer your support to one another. Be childlike with each other while you raise your child, all the while respecting each other's space, likings, memories, passions and sacrifices.

Childhood Memories of Parents

We all have childhood memories that have stayed with us. The first five years of our life form the basis of our future mental health.

We all might have had some good and bad memories while growing up–that must have led to the shaping up of our personalities. Many parents have had bad experiences as a child themselves. They might have been hit by their parents in their childhood, the effects of which are seen when they vent out their anger on their child. If they were sent to boarding schools and did not get to spend much time with their family, there are chances they might struggle with developing a bond with their child. If their own parents had an unhappy marriage, they too might not be very respectful towards their partner in front of their child.

It is very important to not let the negative aspects of your childhood reflect in your parenting. I feel that parents should discuss about the suppressed emotions from their childhood with a counsellor and not suppress them any further to be able to form a stronger bond with their baby and their partner. I believe that as you grow as a parent, you also grow as a couple, and just like the bond between the parent and child should grow stronger, that between the two partners should also strengthen. Hence, all supressed negative emotions—be it from your childhood, your parents or from your marriage—should be released.

Being a parent gives us an opportunity to revisit our childhood—we get an opportunity to play with toys and engage with our baby in ways that we wished we were by our parents. We can explore the perfect balance between our inner child and our adult life gradually as we transition into the new phase of parenthood by letting our inner child come out and bond with our baby. Let your baby know that you are not always strict and can bond with them being the way they are. Doing so, you will become your child's best friend.

Dear Mom and Dad,

We all have a child inside us, and it only comes out in specific situations. Becoming a new parent gives you a great opportunity of bringing out that hidden child in you. One definitely needs to be responsible all the time as a parent, but sometimes while spending time with your baby, allow that child in you to come out and be the baby with your little one. Cherish every memory.

Love,

Dr Mahima Bakshi

14

From First to Second Year

From completing six months of exclusive breastfeeding to feeding them solids, you and your baby have come a long way. It is time for their first birthday. Well, it is a milestone. You should not just be celebrating the first birthday of your little one but also the fact that you successfully managed to pass every transition phase within the first year of motherhood.

Equal parenting not just makes it easy to bring up a child but also makes the child understand how the father is contributing emotionally and physically in raising them. Resonating with the 'push present' culture in western countries, the father should gift something to the mother on every birthday of their child, as she too is achieving new milestones in motherhood with every passing year.

How often do women think of themselves on the first birthday of their child? I totally adore those mothers who probably want to don a costume that's twinning with their child's or get dressed to pamper themselves on their child's first birthday. Why limit it to the first? I suggest that the parents should do something of this sort for at least the first five birthdays of their child, or even beyond if they wish to.

Once the baby crosses their first year, you would start feeling more confident about your parenting. You might even start giving advices to the new mothers and would actually enjoy doing so. As your baby enters the second year of their life, you also need to make changes in your parenting style. The same goes for fathers. The two of you would have to grow as parents and take it easy.

Many babies tend to become picky eaters. Ensure that they are introduced to healthy eating habits right from the very beginning. Discipline your child such that they learn to eat right and on time. Remember to not be very strict because your little one is still a baby and could have many mood swings and be fussy for many reasons. Hence, keep consulting your paediatrician to get the best advice, if need be.

If you are a working mother, you would have understood by now how to strike a balance between taking care of work and your child. You would know what works best for you.

Many new mothers also turn into influencers and some start a new business altogether—becoming a mompreneur. Don't let go of your passion. It's okay to take a break if needed or have moments where you feel guilty. Do what makes you happy and enjoy it. Don't let post-partum depression sink in, and don't overload yourself with stress and pressure. Listen to your body and mind. You need to give equal importance to your health.

While there are some mothers who might want to plan a second baby, others might not at all. I have come across many instances of women ending up with another pregnancy within the first year of delivering their first child. This should be definitely avoided. Talk to your gynaecologist about family planning methods to prevent an unplanned pregnancy.

You would also need to focus on helping your firstborn with their learning at home in the first two years. If you decide to not send them to a day-care facility, then you would have to engage them with a series of activities that they would have been introduced to had they been going to day-care—you can keep them occupied and entertained with touch-and-feel books, blocks, puzzles, art therapy, music and clay dough molding. Children around the age of two also enjoy listening to stories, watching puppets and anything that helps fuel their imagination. Such activities are a better way of helping your baby learn. Many schools have now started using phonetics to introduce alphabet to children. This helps in making the learning process easier.

You should also organize play dates for your baby with others of their age, so that they develop social skills and learn to share. Play dates can also give you the chance to interact with other mothers.

When it comes to breastfeeding, you may continue for the first three years. It also helps in boosting your baby's immune system and helps stimulate the release of oxytocin. Many mothers somehow are not able to lactate. If such is the case with you too, then speak to a lactation expert so that you can continue breastfeeding your child. The baby might start biting your nipple once they start teething. Look for ways to help soothe the pain. You can try using ice packs or lanolin creams on nipples; expressed milk at the end of the feed can also be applied; letting some air circulate around nipples post feed by leaving it open for 5–10 minutes can also be helpful. Remember to unlatch your baby when they bite as it would discourage them from biting your nipples again. You may temporarily use nipple shield during feeds. If nothing seems to help, you can express your milk and feed the baby through cups till the time your nipples are healed and the pain has subsided.

Many new mothers turn into homemakers. My mother, too, became one after which her life became quite monotonous—she would only take care of her family and not herself. It is okay for you to take a Sunday off for yourself to break free from the routine for once. You and your partner can have alternate Sundays to yourselves, such that the other is not expected to do much on that day. Many husbands are of the view that since they only get a Sunday to relax after a hectic week, they should be allowed to enjoy the day all by themselves. Fathers must follow equal parenting and share their Sundays.

Parenting is a continuous learning process. As your child grows, you would also grow as a parent. Learn and grow with your child. It is not just the child that needs constant encouragement for their little achievements, but also the parents. Parents feel the most encouraged when they notice that their parenting has had a positive bearing on their child.

Dear Mom,

As you enter the second year of your parenthood, you would gain confidence in many things. You would probably be sitting and advising your friends and colleagues who have just had a baby. You would feel more experienced. You would now be almost able to manage your time, work and your baby in a more balanced way. However, you would find yourself running around most of the time as your baby would start walking by now. So don't forget to babyproof your house and keep your child's safety in mind as you gradually move into the second year of their life.

Love,

Dr Mahima Bakshi

15

Mindful Parenting

Raising a child can be a huge responsibility, but when shared equally, the load becomes lighter. When both the parents participate equally in parenting, it makes a huge difference in shaping the future of the child. Modern-day parents stand face to face with certain challenges when it comes to parenting.

1. Partners are finding it difficult to take out time for their family.
2. There is a lack of family support, especially when staying in nuclear families.
3. The abundance of information available over the Internet and an easy access to the same confuses the parents who are seeking the right information.

4. There is a mounting social pressure on the parents. They tend to get influenced by what others say or do.
5. The financial stress adds to the trouble. If their jobs are not paying well or if the expenses are skyrocketing, they are bound to be distressed.
6. Demanding careers—usually accompanied with longer working hours—take up their time.
7. Overuse of gadgets and being hooked to social media platforms leave parents with little time to spend with their newborn.

Now, we cannot go back to the old days, running away from the modernity that we have become a part of. However, we can change the way we deal with our problems. Sometimes, I feel that modernization has led us to live for society, stopping us from living for ourselves. If we were to live doing what we liked, we would be more peaceful in our lives. How many of us are actually content with what we have? Our desires are never ending and, hence, we are never able to be content with what we have in life. We have never been able to stop wanting more and cherish what we already have. Modernization has only made us greedier. The race never ends.

The only way for us to be able to experience a feeling of contentment is to practise mindfulness. Let us apply that to get rid of our modern-day parenting challenges.

1. **Lack of time:** Make a conscious effort to take out time for your family—divide your time sensibly between your partner, child and friends. Prioritize your relationships well. No matter how much time you spend at home, make sure it is dedicated entirely to your family and they have your undivided attention.

    When at home, follow specific rules. For example, everyone must eat dinner together on a dinner table; nobody should watch TV or use mobile phones while eating; the dinner time should be utilized in talking to each other; you might go for a walk with the family after dinner. Spend your Sundays at home with your family—you may take them out for a lunch or a movie or play a game together. Avoid attending to office work on Sundays.

2. **Lack of family support:** Sometimes, we have too many expectations from our closed ones, but are not able to express those due to a communication gap. We should be able to express ourselves when we expect or need help from someone. Try to convince your family to help you by telling them about your situation. Talk openly. If they are unable to offer any help, try understanding their reasons, and look for alternate options. You could look for babysitters around you. If that is not doable, then you need to analyse your options again. You or your partner

could choose to work from home or look for a job that allows either of you to stay at home with the baby. Sit down and talk to each other for a solution, rather than cribbing about not getting any help from your family members.
3. **Lack of correct knowledge:** Start reading parenting books as early as possible because you would eventually get busier with your baby and barely find any time to read. Attend antenatal and postnatal workshops by experts. Attend parenting workshops to learn more. Whenever you feel you are unable to cope, seek a counsellor's help. You can also seek group support—talk to other people going through the same phase as yours, so that you don't feel like you are the only one going through it. You can also seek their advice.
4. **Societal pressure:** Every individual is different and so are their lives. Do not go on comparing your life with that of others as you might not be aware of their reality or of their circumstances. Try to be happy with what you do and with what you have. Try not to get influenced by seeing what others are doing or by what others are saying. Use your own mind and follow your own instincts. Get realistic.
5. **Financial pressure:** Once you become parents, you obviously have to take care of new expenses. Choose the hospital where you plan to deliver, the products

that you would use for the baby, the paediatrician and also the school you would send your baby to. Become practical in planning your expenses. If you end up following what others are opting for and not exploring what is actually best suited for you, you might end up burning a hole in your pocket too soon without even realizing. So, plan monthly expenses of your baby according to your savings and earnings.

6. **Demanding careers:** Make the right choices. Many a time I have seen mothers worrying about returning to work when there is no family support in looking after the baby at home. It becomes an act of juggling between the baby and office work. While some decide to take a break from their work till the baby is at least two years old, some start their own business or become entrepreneurs, so that they can have flexible working hours and take care of the baby. Many fathers, too, decide to take a career break to support their wife's career if the latter cannot quit. There are couples who decide to change their house for moving closer to their office—this also helps them cut down on their commuting time so that they can spend some extra minutes with their baby. You must make choices keeping in mind what is more important for you. Figure out what suits you best.

7. **Overuse of gadgets:** It is important to go on a digital detox once in a while. It will help you learn how to control your screen hours and would also be healthy for your mind. Doing so, you will be able to spend more quality time with your baby and give them more attention. Once you reach home, try to keep your phones away. Stay away from using phones on Sundays. Avoid doing any office work at home once you come back. Try to stay off social media platforms for a while as you learn to be new parents. Instead, invest that time learning how to look after your newborn.

Managing challenges as new parents would help you achieve more clarity in your journey of parenthood; you would be able to enjoy raising your baby. Once you start practising mindfulness, you will be able to make the right choices for them, such that they never feel neglected. As your child grows up, there are a few things you should keep in mind.

- Pay attention to your baby when they try to communicate with you, even if they are too young to talk. Respond to them even if they cannot understand whatever you are saying. They like the fact that you are engaging with them.
- Give them the warmth of your touch—hold, carry and cuddle them more often.
- The baby loves your smell as they recognize who

you are—this is true for both the parents. So don't tamper with your natural body smell.
- Spend quality time with your child. They love making eye contacts with you. So, just keep your phones aside when you talk to your baby, when you hold them or play with them.

Both the parents should give their 100 per cent to the baby right from the very beginning. The way you nurture your baby in the early years would define their growth and development. If you feel guilty for not being able to maintain a balance between taking care of your baby and office workload, then try practising mindfulness. Doing so, you will be able to enjoy your time with your baby and also give a 100 per cent at work. However, your baby should be a top priority.

As new parents, you would have to learn to prioritize your baby and make lifestyle changes when required. Avoiding smoking and consumption of alcohol should not just be the rule for the mother but the father too. Changes like these will help you learn to give up on things that are no longer important and healthy for you and your baby. Learn to be with them when they need you.

Dear Mom and Dad,

More than anything else in this world, your baby needs your time and attention. Practising mindfulness might seem to be a small thing but can add so much value to your parenting journey, and make it better for your baby and you. While you might be busy in your life, do not forget to give your time and attention to your baby—that will be your precious gift to them. Keep this in mind to make your parenting journey more memorable.

Love,

Dr Mahima Bakshi

16

Avoiding Another Pregnancy Too Soon

A woman needs time to adapt to the hormonal, physical and emotional changes her body and mind undergoes during pregnancy. Post delivery, too, similar changes occur—she's trying to lose weight, is worried about her skin and hair changing, is coping with post-partum depression, is learning how to feed her baby, is trying to adjust to the sleepless nights and what not. Despite undergoing the hoard of changes, she strives to strike a balance between the new phase of motherhood and her own health.

A woman's own health and physical and emotional well-being should be seen as equally important as that of her baby. Trying to adapt to all the changes can get exhausting.

She might actually want to take a day off.

Post-partum depression can occur at anytime until two years post delivery. Hence, it is not just in the early post-partum period but even the latter part when one should be careful. For working mothers, returning to office once their maternity leave is over can be exhausting as they have to then strike a balance between career and the baby. She would need some time to understand how to find a balance between all her responsibilities and yet be able to take care of herself. She should be able to eventually enjoy her motherhood and her new life. A new mother has quite a lot of things to take care of. Support from family and partner is very important for her to be able to cope through this transition phase. My advice to all new mothers is: 'Go slow, don't overexert yourself with high expectations and take it easy.'

On days when you want to take an off from your duties as a mother, you can seek your partner's help. On such days, you could either go meet your family, friends or get some much needed sleep. Meanwhile, your partner can look after the baby and feed them expressed milk. Thus, partner support and equal parenting remains significant for a couple to share responsibilities and pass through the post-partum depression phase.

These are also important for the new mother when she is struggling to get back in shape, breastfeed the baby, all the while trying to enjoy the new phase of her life. She might take up to two years to adapt to the changes in her life.

My advice to all new mothers is to keep a check on their well-being too—try to avoid another pregnancy too soon. I have known many mothers who ended up with another pregnancy (an unplanned one) within two years of their first delivery. The body is still recovering from the first pregnancy. Mentally, the mother is still trying to figure out how to take care of her firstborn and manage her work. She is still learning how to look after herself and is suffering from sleep deprivation. Under such circumstances, if she turns pregnant again, how will she cope with all the changes all over again, right from the beginning? That's for you to think and imagine.

After the initial post-partum bleeding, also called lochia, you would probably notice that you have not been getting your periods for a while. This would then be followed by irregular periods as you continue breastfeeding, thanks to the lactation hormones. Hence, it becomes tough to calculate your 'safe' or 'unsafe' window to use it as a contraceptive method.

Due to the irregular periods, a woman might not be able to realize that she is pregnant. Hence, following a proper contraceptive method is very important to avoid another pregnancy too soon unless your gynaecologist gives you a go-ahead. So, discuss about family planning methods with your gynaecologist before resuming your sex life.

Resuming Sex Life after Having a Baby

As you deliver and still feel sore everywhere—it could be soreness in the breasts or in the abdomen due to the stitches post C-section or in the perineal area following vaginal birth—you would obviously not be having any urge to engage in any sexual activity. Once you start feeling better, are able to cope better with the lack of sleep and the changes in your lifestyle (all the while trying to keep yourself away from post-partum depression), you would gradually get back your sex drive after a couple of weeks—in some cases, it could be after a few months too.

The partner could help the new mother get back her sex drive—mere hugs and kisses can also help. Respecting the fact that her body has undergone hormonal and physical changes, you can slowly try to bring back your sex life on track once she is ready for it. Avoid rushing into it. Try to make her feel loved and desired by you in every way.

How Soon Is Too Soon?

Women should try to keep a gap of at least two years before planning another baby. Your little one needs your undivided attention during the early years of their life, especially till the time they start going to school. Your body needs about two years to get prepared again to go through another pregnancy and then be ready to manage two kids at the same time. Thus, communicate with your partner, talk to your gynaecologist about it and learn more about the effective contraceptive methods that you can follow while breastfeeding your firstborn.

- **Barrier method:** Couples should use condoms. Discuss this with your doctor. Women too can use condoms. Talk to your gynaecologist to know about it in detail.
- **Withdrawal method:** Pull-out method right before ejaculation is not 100 per cent effective. If the man is unable to withdraw at the right time and if the precum secretion has sperms, it could lead to a pregnancy.
- **Dermal patches:** These are placed subcutaneously and slowly release hormones that act as contraception. Talk to your gynaecologist to find out more about it.
- **Intrauterine device:** In earlier days, Copper-T became a popular contraceptive choice amongst many women, and they would get it removed when they wanted to plan a pregnancy. These days, Mirena is popularly used.
- **Oral contraceptive pills:** They are available in different hormonal combinations and can be used safely while breastfeeding. Talk to your gynaecologist before starting one. They are generally also known as birth control pills.

- **Emergency pills:** These should be avoided when the women is breastfeeding. It should only be kept as an emergency contraceptive option and is also known as morning after pill.
- **Female sterilization surgery or fallopian tube ligation:** Many women also decide to get a surgical sterilization procedure done in case they don't want another pregnancy at all.
- **Vasectomy:** Men, too, can get the surgical sterilization procedure done in case the couple does not want another pregnancy again.

Planning another baby or not is completely a mutual decision of the couple. While some decide to only raise one child, others want to have another baby later in life. Instead of having an unplanned pregnancy, it's better to have an open communication with each other and plan your second baby with the right form of family planning method.

Both the partners should handle the responsibility of avoiding unplanned pregnancy. It's better to avoid an unplanned pregnancy rather than going for medical termination of the pregnancy or abortions. After having your first baby, think of the well-being of the mother and plan the second one accordingly. The first baby should at least be able to enjoy your undivided attention during the first two years of their life.

Dear Mom and Dad,

I have seen many couples get pregnant quite soon after having their first baby. Most of them are barely ready for it. Your firstborn would need your undivided attention in the initial period, especially for the first two years. It can be very exhausting. So keep a gap of at least two years before planning another pregnancy. Your body needs to recover, get back in shape and regain strength. You also need to be mentally prepared to have a second baby. Do not take contraception lightly, and avoid having an unplanned pregnancy. Ensuring an unplanned pregnancy does not occur is the equal responsibility of both the partners.

Love,

Dr Mahima Bakshi

17

Skin and Hair Care

As a new mother, there are many things to take care of in the postnatal period—baby care, breastfeeds, paediatric visits, your struggle with weight loss, etc. In this phase, a new mother tends to forget that the hormonal changes in her body are also affecting her hair and skin.

Many pregnant women enjoy the pregnancy glow and the increased volume of their hair. They can't seem to get enough pictures of themselves to flaunt that glowing skin and crowning glory. There are also those who end up with pregnancy acne and pigmentation as a result of the hormonal changes. Every woman goes through a different set of changes. They should avoid chemical treatment of hair and skin during pregnancy as much as possible. In fact, you can find it written on many skin cream boxes that they are not supposed to be used by pregnant women. So, once you have delivered your baby and have settled into the new phase—I totally believe it takes at least 40 days for a new mother to adapt to this new phase in her life—you can start focusing on skin treatments and even see a dermatologist, if needed.

This doesn't mean that you should not take care of your skin and hair for the first 40 days. Follow your basic skin care routine of cleansing, toning and moisturizing on a daily basis from the second day itself. You might also experience a lot of sweating as a result of breastfeeding and post-partum hormonal changes. So ensure that you keep your skin clean. Hence, I advise new mothers to follow their basic skincare routine twice a day. You can also start using a Vitamin C serum that would help in reducing your pigmentation.

I also suggest new mothers to have a bowl of papaya everyday as it contains certain enzymes and Vitamin A, both of which are very good for skin. Papaya also acts as a great laxative and helps in clearing your bowels. In case of pigmentation, too, papaya face packs can be a great home remedy. So you can apply it once a week. In case of acne, chandan and multaani mitti face packs can come in handy. Apply them once a week to reduce acne spots and scars.

Saunf, ajwain and jeera water is useful for detoxification and is good for the gut as it is a probiotic; it acts as a lactation booster and is also great for a new mother's skin. It is advisable to consume one to two litres of the same on a daily basis. In fact, I have seen new mothers achieve great weight loss results by drinking it. If you want to lose some pregnancy weight, continue consuming the concoction for the next six months to a year.

To reduce dark circles, you could apply some sweet almond oil around your eyes twice a day and massage around your eyes with finger tips to improve the blood circulation. You could also apply cucumber slices for a few minutes while you are treating yourself with some me time to get rid of those puffy eyes. For further relaxation, try stepping out in some early morning sunlight—spending some 20–30 minutes outside would be great for your skin and bones. Don't forget to apply some sunscreen (even when indoors).

Postnatal massages with coconut and olive oil prove to be beneficial in reducing stretch marks. They can be used in improving your skin texture and reducing marks. You could also consult your dermatologist to get rid of them completely. Also remember, you need not stress on losing weight immediately post delivery. Focus on toning your skin with postnatal exercises and massages.

Most pregnant women experience an increased hair growth. However, post delivery, once the pregnancy hormones start decreasing, they start experiencing a reduction in hair growth and even hair fall. Hence, new mothers need to take good care of not just their skin but hair too. A soft head massage with essential oils once or twice a week for 30 minutes before shampooing could be a great way of hydrating your scalp and also helps in boosting the blood circulation to your scalp, improving your hair texture and growth. Regular cleansing of hair is also important in keeping your scalp clean. Hormonal changes in the body and postnatal exercises can cause post-partum sweating. So, keep your scalp clean with a regular mild cleanser that you can use instead of a strong chemical based shampoo. Avoid getting any hair treatments like keratin or smoothening for the first three to four months post delivery. Try to stick to as many home-made remedies as you can.

Ensure a good diet intake. Almonds, walnuts, flax seeds, sunflower seeds, pumpkin seeds, avocado and food items high in zinc and Vitamin E should be consumed on a regular basis. Your gynaecologist would anyway advise you to take iron and calcium supplements for some time after you have given birth. Iron deficiency in new mothers can also lead to a lot of hair fall. So, eat food items like green leafy vegetables, jaggery, dates, raisins, apples, pomegranate, carrots, beetroots on a daily basis. Your hair and skin are made of protein, and proteins in diet help in promoting healthy hair growth and skin regeneration.

Amla juice helps improve the quality of your hair and skin, and also boosts your immunity. Try to add one glass of amla juice mixed with some aloe vera extracts to your diet and consume it on a regular basis. It is also good for

Skin and Hair Care

post-partum weight loss. You could add a spoon of honey and half a slice of lemon to it.

While you enjoy your time with your baby looking after their needs, do not forget to look after your hair and skin too.

Dear Mom,

The post-partum phase can understandably be very exhausting. You might hardly get time to think of your skin and hair care routines. But the more you try to take care of yourself, the healthier you would feel from within. Follow the tips mentioned in the chapter. Allow your hormonal changes to bounce back to the normal. Most of the changes are reversible and we are only trying to help you pamper yourself to feel healthier and fitter.

Love,

Dr Mahima Bakshi

18
Rediscovering Your Inner Goddess

As you transition into the new phase of your life, you need not lose your identity. As you learn to grow into motherhood, remember it is an ongoing process. You will always be surrounded by responsibilities of your baby. Just as your baby grows, you would also grow everyday as a parent. Motherhood is a fulltime task. Hence, participation and support from husbands play an important role in helping the woman rediscover her inner goddess.

I strongly believe that womanhood doesn't cease to exist once motherhood begins. Becoming a mother does not mean that you can no longer enjoy your womanhood. You need to just learn to do your new tasks with the support of your partner. Ask them for help when you need, don't hesitate. Let the community help and support you—become a part of support groups. Let your organization help you. Talk to your boss when your maternity leave is about to end. Let your in-laws and baby bond with each other. Let your body take a day off when you need it. As you seek support, try to rediscover yourself as a woman and reconnect with the woman you were.

Allow yourself at least a year's time to be able to strike a balance, get back to your pre-pregnancy body shape and to resettle into your relationship with your partner. Start doing things that you once liked to. Do things that would help you feel like a woman again and not just a mother. Spend time with your husband. Take yourself out for shopping; go for some pampering at the salon. You can even hang out with your friends or go on a trip with them for a weekend while your partner can take care of the baby and bond with them. Talk and discuss about things that are not just related to your baby.

Fathers, you too can have some space when you need it. You can go on for a boys' night-out, but obviously not immediately after your wife has given birth, as she would need you. Once she starts feeling better, shows no signs of post-partum depression and is able to start celebrating her womanhood again with your support, you can start taking out time for yourself too.

Together, the two of you can rediscover your love and bond as a couple. You can work on recreating that love and magic in your relationship. Go for staycations, try cooking together, go for dinner dates and plan movie nights to bring back that spark in your relationship. Reminisce the romance and put an effort to bond again as a couple. Once you start getting into that happy space again in your own life, you would have lesser disagreements, you would feel good about yourselves again and be able to make each other feel good too. Compliment each other on how they look, enjoy each other's company and respect the efforts that the other is putting in.

Rediscovering yourself after becoming a mother is very important to lead a balanced and happy life ahead. Hence, as much as we advise you to spend time learning everything about parenthood, your baby and your well-being, eventually you need to get back to rediscovering yourself too. You need to boost those happy hormones. Ask for help when you need it and remember that talking is the most effective therapy. Self-realization is the biggest tool to one's wellness. Nobody can help you until you are willing to help yourself. Show dedication and commitment not just for your baby, but yourself too, so that you can bring out the woman in you who probably gets hidden behind the mother that you become. Let your partner help you. Together the two of you can not only become wonderful parents but also a great couple. Husbands need to be more sensitive towards their wives and understand that their body goes through physical and emotional changes during pregnancy.

Your one step towards taking care of her would help her take 10 steps towards taking care of herself. Help her in rediscovering herself, remind her of the things that she used to enjoy doing, remind her of how wonderful she's doing as a new mother, surprise her by cooking her favourite dish or by ordering her favourite food on a date night. Offer to babysit for a weekend so that she can spend time on rediscovering herself.

Seek help from a counsellor if needed. At times, when a couple can't manage to find that balance to rediscover their relationship once they become parents, family counselling comes in handy.

Dear Mom,

You are strong. You are powerful. You are beautiful. You are incredible. Your inner goddess is waiting for you to be appreciated, to be rediscovered and to be praised. Let her get what she deserves. Continue to believe in your dreams, don't give up on those. Continue to give wings to your dreams, let your inner goddess fly high. Be who you are, don't let your individual identity get lost. Support your inner goddess and see the magic happen. Keep reminding her that you are taking care of her. As much as your newborn, she too needs you.

Love,

Dr Mahima Bakshi

Afterword

Couples are getting exposed to modern-day challenges like career goals, late marriages, difficulty in conceiving and lack of support from family. This book will help them find solutions to the challenges that they face as new parents and evolve in their new role. With this work, I hope to help new mothers take better care of their newborn, and be able to rediscover themselves with the support of their partners.

This book also aims at aiding new mothers in taking care of their well-being, so that they can enjoy their motherhood and prevent post-partum depression. The new fathers who read this book would be able to be more involved in taking care of their wife and their baby. They would be able to learn about sharing responsibilities and equal parenting. I hope that I am able to bring a revolution in parenting, which would positively impact the development of the baby

Afterword

and their growth in the early years.

I believe that we cannot empower women around us without men supporting women and similarly we cannot empower the new mothers to take care of themselves and the baby without fathers supporting mothers. The only solution to the modern-day challenges of parenting is equal parenting. Hence, I hope to spread more awareness about how important it is for a new mother to take care of herself post delivery, for fathers to take care of their wife and the baby and for the couple to grow as parents with equal parenting.

The two of you together can give the best to your baby during the early years of their life. Happy mothers make happy babies, and fathers can help in increasing their happiness by being equally involved in taking care of both of them. Let your baby get the most from your parenting during their early years. Make lifestyle changes once your baby arrives as they tend to be observational learners. Giving breastmilk to your baby is the most beneficial choice you can make for them.

Involvement of both the partners is crucial right from the pregnancy phase. But there are certain things that the baby demands only from the mother—like the mother's touch, voice, smell and her breastmilk. After the mother, it is the father's voice that they get to hear the most and his touch that they get to feel the most. Hence, fathers should be encouraged to bond with the baby during pregnancy, be it through the womb, so that the baby gets familiar with the father too. Let your baby know that both of you are equally excited and involved in preparing for their arrival.

Acknowledgements

Just the way I tried to help pregnant women with my book *Birthing Naturally*, through this book, I wish to help women take care of themselves after giving birth.

I would like to thank Rupa Publications and Rudra Narayan Sharma for giving me this opportunity for my second book, *Empowering You Beyond Birthing*. I would also like to thank Sakschi Verma for working on my book.

I would also like to thank all my patients—pregnant and new moms—who have always inspired me to do more for the mothers in society. I would like to thank my mother, who has always been the reason why I could work in the area of maternal child wellness. I would like to thank my childhood friend Dr Isha Kriplani and her mother Dr Alka Kripalani, who have always been there to support me for all my initiatives. I would like to thank my dad for letting me pursue my passion and for believing in his daughters and never treating us any less than sons. I would like to thank my sisters too.

And most importantly my pet shih-tzu, Zara, who would show her patience when her walks would clash with my writing time.

I would like to thank all the organizations who supported my passion and gave me an opportunity to work for them. I would like to thank all those obstetricians and gynaecologists who believed in my passion and supported me for my work—Dr Suchitra Pandit, Dr Hrishikesh Pai, Dr Alka Kripalani, Dr Pranathi Reddy, Dr Meenakshi Ahuja, Dr Nisha Kapoor and everyone else I have worked with.

I would also like to thank all the paediatricians who supported my passion—Dr Anupam Sibal, Dr Ramesh Kancharla, Dr Dinesh Chirla and all others who helped me learn and grow under their guidance.

I would also like to thank Dr Ali Irani for always guiding me and mentoring me to reach where I am today.

I would also like to thank *Woman's Era* magazine for always supporting me for all my initiatives and organizations like Manav Rachna University, Fiama by ITC, Niine India, etc., for always backing me in my cause.

I would like to dedicate this book to all the new mothers who looked for postnatal support in me, who believed in my help.I would also like to dedicate this book to all the expecting and new moms who have participated in 'Birthing

Acknowledgements

Naturally Queen,' who helped me spread awareness on maternal mental health by supporting me to empower more mothers around us.